AuctionWatch.com's
Official
Guide to Online
Buying
and
Selling

Send Us Your Comments:

To comment on this book or any other PRIMA TECH title, visit our reader response page on the Web at www.prima-tech.com/comments.

How to Order:

For information on quantity discounts, contact the publisher: Prima Publishing, P.O. Box 1260BK, Rocklin, CA 95677-1260; (916) 787-7000. On your letterhead, include information concerning the intended use of the books and the number of books you want to purchase.

AuctionWatch.com's
Official
Guide to Online
Buying
and
Selling

**AuctionWatch.com
& Dennis L. Prince**

A DIVISION OF PRIMA PUBLISHING

A Division of Prima Publishing

Prima Publishing and colophon and Fast & Easy are registered trademarks of Prima Communications, Inc. PRIMA TECH is a trademark of Prima Communications, Inc., Roseville, California 95661.

The Complete Auction Management Solution and Buy Anywhere. Sell Anywhere. Start Here. are registered trademarks of AuctionWatch.com

Important: Prima Publishing cannot provide software support. Please contact the appropriate software manufacturer's technical support line or Web site for assistance.

Prima Publishing and the author have attempted throughout this book to distinguish proprietary trademarks from descriptive terms by following the capitalization style used by the manufacturer.

Information contained in this book has been obtained by Prima Publishing from sources believed to be reliable. However, because of the possibility of human or mechanical error by our sources, Prima Publishing, or others, the Publisher does not guarantee the accuracy, adequacy, or completeness of any information and is not responsible for any errors or omissions or the results obtained from use of such information. Readers should be particularly aware of the fact that the Internet is an ever-changing entity. Some facts may have changed since this book went to press.

ISBN: 0-7615-2999-3

Library of Congress Catalog Card Number: 00-106648

Printed in the United States of America

00 01 02 03 04 II 10 9 8 7 6 5 4 3 2 1

Publisher:
Stacy L. Hiquet

Marketing Manager:
Judi Taylor Wade

Marketing Coordinator:
Jennifer Breece

Managing Editor:
Sandy Doell

Acquisitions Editor:
Stacy L. Hiquet

Project Editor:
Estelle Manticas

Technical Reviewer:
Chris Aloia

Copy Editor:
Hilary Powers

Interior Layout:
Scribe Tribe

Cover Design:
Prima Design Team

Indexer:
Jonna VanHoose Dinse

For Diane, Eric, and Alex – the family that is my *offline* passion.

Acknowledgments

When AuctionWatch approached me to write this book, I was nothing less than honored to take on the task. They are a company of true professionals and auction advocates in every sense of the words. My sincere thanks to Bill Meyer, AW Director of Editorial Content, for working with me to bring this book to print; he has an energy for auctions that is as motivating as it is refreshing.

Special thanks to Rodrigo Sales and Mark Dodd, the founders of AuctionWatch, not only for providing the Foreword to this book but more so for their original vision and drive to build the best and most comprehensive online auction advocacy site.

And not to overlook many of the other fine folks at AuctionWatch who have helped bring this project to fruition: Millie Lee, Dan Neary, Hetal Soni, Cynthia Cooper, Jason Stein, and Jeff Clementz. My thanks to you all.

Of course thanks to my publisher, Stacy Hiquet, for recognizing the timeliness of this book and her support of it every step of the way. Then, rounding up the usual suspects, I give thanks to my technical editor, Chris Aloia, and copy editor, Hilary Powers, for staying with me on this third endeavor into online auctions. They've stood by me and have provided exceptional input and insight on my past three books—and I hope they'll continue with me for however many more are on the horizon.

And, of course, big thanks to Estelle Manticas, my project editor and all-around sounding board for anything and everything that was on my mind during the development of this book.

Last, but certainly not least, I must acknowledge the community of members at AuctionWatch. If you, the reader, haven't yet dropped in or joined up with them in AW Message Center, you really should. These folks know auctions, and how. My thanks to all of them for keeping the conversation lively and for keeping online auctioning both a pleasure and an opportunity.

Dennis L. Prince is a business professional with a background in both technical (computer) applications and corporate procurement principles. As a long-time Internet user and online auction enthusiast, he has written extensively about the online auction industry, serving up instruction and commentary in advocacy for the auction communities. He is also a regular editorial contributor to AuctionWatch.com as well as the author of *Auction This!* (November 1999), and *Online Auctions @ eBay* (September 1999), both published by Prima Tech.

Contents

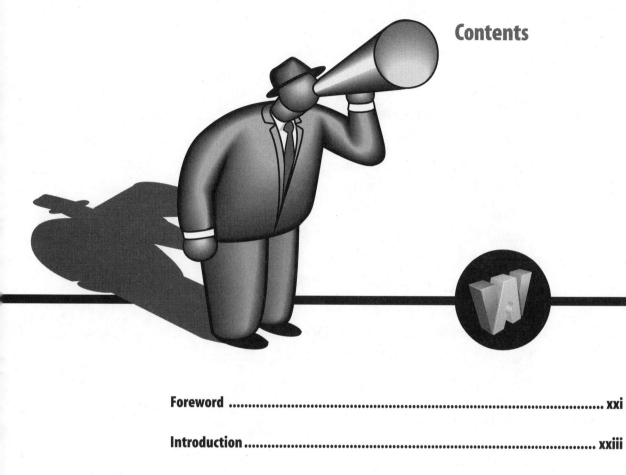

Part III   The Evolution of Your Business   215

Foreword

Last year, Mark Dodd and I began to execute on a powerful vision, one that since has empowered businesses, both big and small, to harness the unparalleled sales potential of the Internet. We recognized the need for an application platform that would enable businesses to effectively introduce their products to the online marketplace and become active players in the new economy.

For Mark and I, this need spelled opportunity—the opportunity to pull together a talented team and build a powerful suite of online and offline sales management tools with which businesses could achieve hitherto unimaginable levels of success and prosperity.

In the last 12 months, we have seized upon this opportunity, transforming AuctionWatch.com into the leading auction services company on the Internet—with over 150 employees as far away as Bucharest, Romania and as close as San Bruno, California. We have also attracted one of the most dedicated and talented engineering and product marketing teams in the industry and launched a vast array of critical buyer and seller services, from Auction

Manager and Auction Manager Pro to Universal Search, Universal Registration, and AuctionWatch Appraisals.

Today, AuctionWatch.com is one of the Internet's leading e-commerce platforms for online businesses, with more than 500,000 registered users and over 4.5 million unique visitors a month. During the first half of this year alone, online merchants have sold more than a quarter of a billion dollars in merchandise using AuctionWatch.com's Auction Manager tool set, which includes Auction Manager Pro, Inventory Management, Customer Relationship Management, and Post Sale Management, among other professional listing services. And consider this: Over 12 percent of all online auctions on eBay, the World's leading consumer auction site are listed using AuctionWatch.com's services. Sellers use our services to create and manage over 2 million auctions every month, making us realize that our objective of empowering online sellers is met daily.

Buyers are validating our services, as well. Our Universal Search service, which provides users with the latest auction and fixed price listings on the Net, helps millions of buyers efficiently locate items available for sale each month. And just think, only a year ago, AuctionWatch.com was an industry favorite on the merits of its Image Hosting service and Message Center, now only two services out of the vast array we provide. As we improve and expand our existing buyer and seller services and partner with other leading e-commerce and e-business companies, it is truly an exciting time to be part of the AuctionWatch.com community.

Through all this growth and change, we are proud to say that AuctionWatch.com's core mission really has not changed. From our earliest, formative discussions, Mark and I have always wanted to provide buyers and sellers with the tools and information that will help them help themselves, fuel their online ambitions, consider new horizons, and broaden their interpretation of success. Although, as with any start-up, some of our services have taken new directions, a commitment to the success of our members' online businesses still drives all our developmental decisions. In short, we are empowering people to *buy anywhere* and to *sell anywhere*.

That's why we were delighted to participate in the creation and sponsorship of *AuctionWatch.com's Official Guide to Online Buying and Selling* with award winning publisher Prima Tech, which has already published two highly-regarded and successful online auction guides (*Auction This* and *Online Auctions at eBay: Bid With Confidence, Sell With Success*) by recognized expert and advocate Dennis L. Prince. Like all AuctionWatch.com's products, this comprehensive, easy-to-use guide supports our main objective—empowering users so that they can maximize their potential and realize business goals they did not know were attainable.

I'm convinced this unique handbook for novices and online professionals alike will become the online sellers' bible. Like an editor's style guide or master chef's favorite cookbook, this is one reference book that won't collect dust on your shelf—you'll use it! We expect that auction pros will refer to it again and again to answer critical questions quickly and concisely in the heat of an important transaction and that its worn pages will never be far from their computer.

As you read on and shift your online business into high gear, remember the learning does not begin and end here. The real opportunity continues at AuctionWatch.com.

With that in mind, we highly recommend that you explore the enclosed CD-ROM, featuring AW's downloadable bulk lister Auction Manager Pro. This indispensable listing and inventory application will open your eyes to a new set of business possibilities. Once you've tried out our services, drop us a line and let us know what you think.

Thanks for sharing our passion and good luck with your online auction business.

Rodrigo Sales, Co-founder and CEO

Mark Dodd, Co-founder and Vice President of Product Development

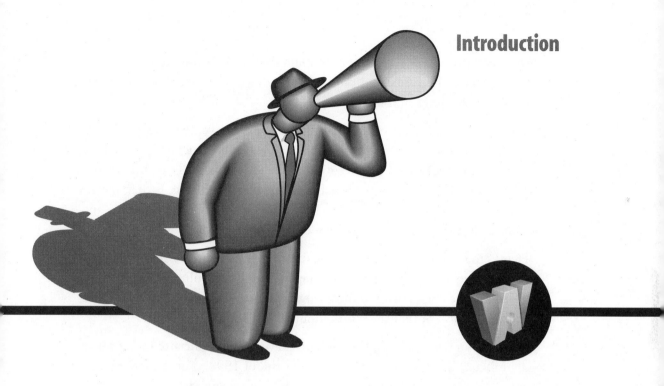

Welcome auction enthusiasts! Online auctions don't need much introduction these days. Though there was a time when the term evoked blank stares or raised eyebrows, online auctions have quickly carved a place in many folks' daily lives. In fact, they've nearly achieved the same household status as the Internet, that other once-mysterious tech-head realm.

Today, going online is as natural as going to your refrigerator. The Internet has brought millions of people together and has proven itself to be an undeniably valuable resource for news, information, and money-making opportunities. With personal computers becoming as commonplace as toasters and TVs, practically everyone and anyone can power up and log on to the new land of plenty: the World Wide Web.

Why Online Auctions?

Without a doubt, online auctions have become a mainstay of our ever-emerging new economy. (*E*-economy? *E-conomy*? Whatever. You know what I mean.)

Originally presented as a sort of hobby and Internet experiment back in 1994, auctions have blossomed and morphed into one of the most compelling new ways to do business in the digital age.

Online auctions have proven themselves to be effective, low-overhead alternatives to traditional buying and selling venues. Online auctions are enabling everyone from CEOs at major corporations to Mom and Pop at the corner store to tap the power and potential of online merchandising. Face it: online, everyone has an equal chance to claim their piece of the pie and online auctions are just the dessert that everyone's been hungry for.

Thanks to the boundless space of the Internet, traders from around the globe can buy and sell wherever and whenever they like. Online auctions never close—they're open 24/7 and there's always a buzz of activity. The world loves online auctions, of that there is no doubt.

And the numbers are in: online auctions have captured the attention of literally millions of people worldwide. By the end of 1999, online auctions were recognized as a $4.5 billion industry—that's up from $1.6 billion in 1998 and with a projected earnings of $19 billion by 2003 (Source: Forrester Research). Online auctions are no fad, no fluke, no flash-in-the-pan venture. Wall Street took note of online auction companies when sites like eBay were recording phenomenal growth and 3-for-1 stock splits only months after their IPO listing. Since then, many major online ventures such as Amazon.com, Yahoo!, and Fairmarket have jumped into the auction arena, each having raised eyebrows and stock prices as a result.

Online auctions are a hit; they're hip, they're happening, and they're here to stay.

Welcome to AuctionWatch: The Complete Auction Management Solution

Upon its initial launch in July 1998, AuctionWatch.com established itself as the auction enthusiast's advocate, taking an impartial, in-depth, and occasionally hard-edged approach to issues and events in the online auction arena. Poised to serve the serious (and sometimes just curious) auction-goer, AuctionWatch.com has made itself the most referred and most trusted online auction utility site. In August 1999, AuctionWatch.com received $9.6 million in venture capital, then secured another $27.8 million in June 2000, all of which has enabled the site to significantly increase its offerings of cutting-edge user tools and indispensable editorial content.

Why an AuctionWatch Book?

First, understand AuctionWatch.com's mission:

"To be the online auction community's definitive and unbiased source for services, resources, and information. Whether you're a beginner or someone who makes their living buying and selling online, AuctionWatch.com is designed to meet all your online auction needs."

AuctionWatch has been well placed and markedly successful in providing assistance to millions of auction-goers. Whether complete newcomers to the fray or seasoned auction veterans, visitors find that AuctionWatch.com is serving up tools and techniques everyone and anyone can use to their ultimate success. For their strategic positioning, forward thinking development, and commitment to make online auctioning easier and more effective for everyone, AuctionWatch.com is the recognized leader in online auction services and support.

And the book. In response to many requests, AuctionWatch.com decided that a "desk reference" was a tool people wanted but couldn't find. Again taking the lead in auction advocacy, AuctionWatch—in cooperation with Prima-Tech—now presents this easy-to-use guidebook to help auction enthusiasts truly wrap their hands around the kind of information they need day in and day out as they navigate the auction spaces. By no means is this book a replacement for AuctionWatch.com's online services. Rather, it is a companion to AuctionWatch.com—one that gives you yet more information and a significant edge in the online auction realm.

What's in This Book?

Information. Fast-paced and rapid-fire information is what awaits you in these pages. This book is designed for those auction-goers who are serious about their auctioning and need to minimize their time and effort and maximize their results. Understanding that, this book provides tips, tactics, and techniques that can be rapidly acquired, quickly absorbed, and immediately applied. You'll find information presented in logical progression and in a format that takes you to the information you need at the moment you need it.

What kind of information awaits you? Here's a quick preview.

Part 1: Getting Started and Brushing Up Your Online Auction Knowledge

In this opening section, find a quick, yet informative, recap of some of the basics of online auctions and auctioning. How to sort through the auction sites and auction formats, how to determine where to buy or sell, how to engage in the activity, and how to pull it all together to get organized and get involved. For some readers, this might be old news, but don't be so sure you know it all—check your understandings, check your assumptions, and be sure your view is up to date.

Part 2: Polishing Your Auction Presence

And just how will you stand out in the crowd? This section offers the insight and advice that helps you get your auctions noticed—how to sell like a pro, how to be sure what you sell is not questionable, and how you can establish inventory and expense controls to keep your budding business in the black.

Part 3: The Evolution of Your Business

Your business is this book's business, and this section will guide you into the ways and means of climbing the free-enterprise ladder. Here you'll find sure-fire methods to market your business, to ensure you're customer driven, to take advantage of financial and legal benefits of running a business, and how to go beyond cyberspace and the home office to take your business in directions you may never have considered.

More Help Is Just a Click Away

As a special feature, you'll find an occasional signal that steers you directly to the AuctionWatch.com Web site. Remember, AuctionWatch is your hub for auction news and services that help all auction-goers make the most of their efforts.

As you read through this book, you'll encounter this special element:

AuctionWatch.com has more!

At this signal you'll be directed to exclusive AuctionWatch.com features and information that support the discussion at hand.

Service Highlight

At this signal you'll find information about special AuctionWatch tools that will help you with the auction management process.

If it's a discussion about keeping current with online auction developments, you'll be directed to AuctionWatch.com's online news area via its unique URL. If the topic is the use of auction counters, you'll be given the quick path to AuctionWatch.com's services section where you can get your own counters to use in your auctions. Remember, this is a book that works *with* the AuctionWatch.com site and will work *for* you.

And don't forget to keep an eye out for the *Key Watch Points*. You'll find them at the end of every chapter and they'll sum up the most salient features of the discussion and will help you make sure you've got a grasp on the information.

Do You Have Questions or Comments?

The world of online auctions is fluid, to say the least. New developments occur every day and AuctionWatch.com is there to analyze and disseminate them to you. However, you may well have questions that haven't been specifically covered here. Perhaps you want deeper explanation about a concept you'll read about. Maybe you'd just like to share an auction experience or observation. Or, you might just want to contact someone and say "thanks for the help."

As we are always at your service, feel free to contact either the folks at AuctionWatch.com or the author directly with your input, revelations, and requests. Here's how:

Write to AuctionWatch.com via e-mail: support@auctionwatch.com.

Write to the author via e-mail: dlprince@bigfoot.com.

PART I

Getting Started

and Brushing Up Your

Online Auction

Knowledge

CHAPTER 1

Step into the Parlor: Understanding the Online Auction Marketplace

Level:	*Beginner*
Reader:	*Buyer, Seller, Interested Bystander*

I f online auctions are a new territory to you, fear not. Many have gone before you and most have found online auctions to be a fun and rewarding way to exchange goods online in a "dynamic pricing environment"—in which the price is determined by how much people are willing to bid. But as with any new endeavor there's a bit of background knowledge you should have under your belt from the get-go. This will be the information that helps you develop your eventual stride and get the most out of your efforts.

If you're new to the cyber-parlor, take your time with this introduction before you jump into the world of online auctions. If you've been lurking about the auctions but haven't yet joined in, why not? If it's because you felt you're not up to speed with your peers, this chapter will give you a solid foundation on which to start building. And if you're a seasoned auction-goer, then let this chapter be simply a reaffirmation of what you already know (or *think* you know, but aren't 100 percent sure of). Whatever your need, start at the start, right here, right now.

AuctionWatch.com has more!

If you're new to online auctions, read AW's "Beginner's Guide to Online Auctions," at

http://www.auctionwatch.com/awdaily/gettingstarted/index.html

This guide not only helps you get a better handle on auction basics, it also serves as a great introduction to AuctionWatch.com.

Alphabet Soup: Dynamic Pricing Venues (P2P, B2C, B2B)

Though you may have had your fill of acronyms, fending off everything from *ATM* to *Y2K*, the fact is you'll encounter many more in the online auction arena. Don't worry—they're just easy little monikers that quickly describe the different auction venues you'll be frequenting.

AuctionWatch.com has more!

AuctionWatch.com has catalogued hundreds of auction sites in its Online Auction Site Directory. Check it out at http://www.auctionwatch.com/directory/

P2P (Person-to-Person) Auctions

Just like the name says, these are auction sites that help everyday people find and sell items. Here's a quick summary of what they're all about.

- From an abacus to a xylophone, whatever you're looking for (or looking to unload), the P2P venue should be your first stop.

- P2P sites are the most popular of the online venues, especially among collectors.

- P2P sites have a local sale feel about them: they're casual and friendly.

- P2P sites embody one of the purest forms of free enterprise, enabling regular people to freely roam about buying and selling in an open marketplace that changes from day to day.

- The biggest site and most emulated formula for successful P2P auctions has to be eBay, though other sites—Yahoo Auctions, Amazon Auctions, and Auctions.com—are also among the favorites.

B2C (Business-to-Consumer) Auctions

These are the sites that offer manufacturers' closeouts, overstock, or refurbished goods at lower-than-retail prices. They're big favorites with lots of people.

- The first-ever online auction was of the B2C variety (Onsale.com, back in 1994).

- B2C sites are typically strong in electronics, computers, housewares, jewelry, sporting goods, or event tickets (but there's much more out there).

- B2C auctions are the preference of many auction-goers because most sales come with solid merchant and manufacturer guarantees, warranties, and other such buyer protections.

- If you're looking for mainstream goods at less-than-mainstream prices, look to B2C auctions.

Service Highlight

AuctionWatch.com's Universal Search product allows consumers and businesses to search hundreds of C2C, B2C, and B2B marketplaces for both consumer merchandise and capital assets. Find it at http://www.auctionwatch.com/usearch/

B2B (Business-to-Business) Venues

Note the word *venue* here. B2B players aren't always auction-oriented. They now play a much larger role in e-commerce.

- In B2B, there are many dynamic pricing venues that offer goods and services directly from one business (a manufacturer or software application provider) to another (a new or established business concern that's looking for new ways to acquire goods, equipment, or services) in which "bids" are made to determine the final value.

- Many B2B venues act as "facilitators" or "aggregators," their focus being on helping businesses reach more customers, develop new markets, and increase their financial bottom line.

- The B2B sites are frequently entitled to a share of the end business's profits (either percentage or transaction-based).

- Unless you're a large-scale business, or looking to become one, B2B is probably not the way to go.

AuctionWatch.com has more!

Need an introduction to the B2B marketplace? See AW's in-depth feature, "Making Sense of B2B," at http://www.auctionwatch.com/usearch/

High-end Auctions

OK, so it's not an acronym, but high-end auctions—those traditional parlors of auction lore—have made the migration to the online realm and are proving successful in their cyber-endeavors.

- Traditional auction houses, such as Sotheby's, Christies, Butterfields, and Sloans, have also developed an online presence.

- More and more, high-end auction houses are staging actual online auctions (with online bidding enabled).

- Frequently, though, high-end auction sites are used for previewing an upcoming land-based auction (and if you can't attend in person, you can submit absentee bids).

AuctionWatch.com has more!

See AW's online reviews of high-end auction sites Sothebys.com and eBay Great Collections at

http://www.auctionwatch.com/awdaily/reviews/sothebys.html

http://www.auctionwatch.com/awdaily/reviews/greatcollections.html

Auction Format Fundamentals

You've got the acronyms, now get familiar with the different auction formats you'll encounter. As with the traditional brick-and-mortar (or barnyard) auctions, online auctions support different methods and means by which items are offered, bid upon, and purchased. Online auctions haven't developed all the different variations that you could encounter in real-life (RL) auctions, but there are still plenty of formats of which to keep track.

Straight Auction

This is the traditional auction, that is, the kind of auction everybody thinks of first, where a single item is offered at an opening bid price.

- Bidders successively increment the high bid until the last bid has been cast (either because other bidders have dropped out or a preset auction duration has elapsed).

- The high bidder honors the final bid price and the seller honors the sale at that price.

- You might hear straight auctions referred to as *ascending price* or *absolute* auctions.

Reserve Price Auction

This is a straight auction with a bit of a catch: the seller establishes a *reserve price*—that is, sets the lowest price he or she will accept for the item.

- The starting bid may well be less than the reserve price (a common practice to entice bidders to begin the bidding), but the reserve price must be met or surpassed during the course of bidding or the seller does not have to sell.

- For sellers, the reserve price helps protect their investment or their view of the value of an item.

- Bidders, however, don't typically like the idea of a "hidden" minimum selling price.

AuctionWatch.com has more!

Need further explanation of reserve price auctions? See AW's online tip, Understanding Reserve Auctions, at http://www.auctionwatch.com/awdaily/ tipsandtactics/sel-reserve.html

Dutch Auction

Perhaps the most perplexing format, Dutch auctions are used to sell off multiple units of the same item at the same time.

- Bidders can bid on one or more of the units being offered.

- If 10 units are offered but 20 bidders cast bids, the highest bidders will take the 10 units when the auction ends. That doesn't mean that 10 of the bidders are sure to get items, though—if the highest bidders wanted multiple units, their high bids secure them the number of units they wanted, with the remainder of units going to the next highest bidders until all units are spoken for.

- The lowest successful bid price is the price that *all* bidders will pay. That is, if the bidder with, say, the fifth-highest bid is the one who secures the last item, the other four winning bidders pay the same lowest winning bid amount as that fifth-highest bidder.

- Dutch auctions are often confused with *Yankee* auctions—Yankee rules state that all winning bidders must pay the winning bid price they offered, which means all winning bidders could end up paying different prices at the auction's close.

- Most people need to go through a Dutch auction a few times before they feel at ease with the format. They *are* a bit difficult to understand at first.

AuctionWatch.com has more! _____

Need further explanation of Dutch auctions? See AW's online tip Understanding Dutch/Yankee Auctions, at http://www.auctionwatch.com/awdaily/ tipsandtactics/sel-reserve.html

Fixed Price or Buy-it-Price Auction

Looking to avoid the bidding process? If so, here's your ticket.

- This type of auction features an immediate buy-it price, which gives an interested buyer the chance to exclaim "I'll pay that price!"

- If the seller agrees and the buy-it price hasn't been surpassed by any previous bidding, the auction can be ended and the buyer pays the seller the buy-it price.

- This format is most prevalent at B2C auctions where multiple units of "inventory" can support these sorts of direct sales.

Reverse Auction

If you're looking to turn the tables on the same old bidders-competing-for-one-item routine, put the *sellers* in competition with one another by using a reverse auction format.

- Prospective buyers post the sorts of items or services they're looking for, sometimes with a target price.

- Sellers (merchants or service providers) who can provide the product or service will bid against one another to "win" the sale.

- Products that are good candidates for reverse auctions include vacation packages, automobiles, insurance, and even home mortgages.

- Reverse auctions became a hot trend late in 1999 with seemingly every business that was direct-selling or auctioning items wanting a piece of the reverse auction market.

- One site, eWanted.com, coined the term "upside-down auctions" just to separate itself from its competition.

AuctionWatch.com has more!

See AW's online review of popular reverse auction site eWanted.com at http://www.auctionwatch.com/awdaily/reviews/ewanted.html

Descending Price Auction

A descending price auction is very much like a reverse auction and, in fact, is the true format of the original Dutch auction. Pay attention.

- A "lot" of identical items is offered at an established bid price.

- The price is then lowered in successive decrements until bidders step forward to claim one (or more) at the present price.

- Often, bidders will all wait for a generally accepted price point to be reached (such as a wholesale value perhaps) before bidding.

- Once the target price is reached, one bidder bids and the rest usually clamor to jump in immediately.

- The bidding is typically quite fast once the target price is met and the entire lot is usually snapped up within moments.

Exchange

Not any sort of "customer returns desk," an *Exchange* is one of the newer formats where buyers and sellers post "orders" to buy or sell items. (New to the online auction world, anyway—Amex and the other stock exchanges have been at it for years, right?)

- Participants state prices they're willing to pay or prices at which they're willing to sell (depending upon their business situation).

- When a buy/sell price match is made (by programmatic matching), an exchange is begun.

- The seller and buyer work together to complete the exchange.

- This format is significantly more complex than most other auctions you'll encounter, but it's a compelling methodology that deserves a good look.

Group Buying

It gets better—some sites will lower the prices of items as more buyers show interest.

- With group buying, the more units that are bid on, the lower the price becomes for the entire group of bidders.

- Bidders actually cooperate on driving the price down as opposed to competing to drive the price up.

Classifieds

Not really an auction, but you'll find classified sales online at some venues (such as Excite!) as well as within the various newsgroups of the Usenet. Someone's selling something. Someone's interested in buying it. Bingo! A fast deal is done. It's that simple.

More Than One Place: Different Sites, Different Delights

Variety is good and variety is what you'll find at online auctions. Not only will you find variety *within* a particular site, but you'll find that the sites themselves vary their offerings, ranging from the "one site offers all" approach to specialized focus that serves specific customer tastes.

General Auctions

These are the sites that offer seemingly everything, including the kitchen sink.

- Whether you're looking for useful items, new and used goods, collectibles, automobiles, or any kind of crazy doo-dad you might possibly want to own or desire to unload, general auctions are where everything's up for bid and anything could show up next.

- Most frequently, general auctions are of the P2P variety spawned when ol' George and Martha cleaned out the attic, back bedroom, or garage.

- Expect to also find some merchants (small or large) who are using general auctions as a new sales venue.

Merchant Auctions

These are your B2C variety venue in which retailers and wholesalers are liquidating their inventories.

- These sites have been highly successful in allowing businesses to move merchandise quickly with very little overhead compared to traditional brick-and-mortar clearance sales.

- Merchant auctions are typically a good place for first-time auction-goers to get their feet wet, largely because the merchant sites are big on site security, customer satisfaction, and merchandise guarantees.

- P2P sites can't always measure up to these merchant site standards of customer satisfaction and merchandise guarantees (at P2P sites, such sales policies can and will vary from seller to seller).

Niche Auctions

Niche auctions serve a specific buyer (or seller) by catering to specific types of goods.

- Commodities like pottery, comic books, musical instruments, fine art, Internet domain names, and various others have brought enough interest and traffic to support their own specialized auction sites.

- For folks with specific tastes, niche auctions are among the best places to find high-quality and authentic goods, informed traders, and an overall support structure that understands the specific needs, desires, and concerns of the niche auction-goer.

Charity Auctions

Charity auctions are another of the most traditional types of auctions. When it comes to raising funds, auctions have been a terrific tool for bringing in money. Now, they're being conducted regularly on the Internet.

- Most often, the goods at charity auctions are donated, further lowering the cost to the auction coordinators and allowing for more money to go to the charity directly.

- Online, charity auctions have been quite successful. You can find charity auctions at almost any auction site; eBay, Yahoo!, and Amazon have all hosted charity auctions at one time or another.

AuctionWatch.com has more!

See AuctionWatch.com's investigation of charity auction sites, Eye on Charity Auctions, at http://www.auctionwatch.com/awdaily/features/charity/index.html

- Some charity auction sites inventory and offer the items for bid, then coordinate the transaction.

- Some charity auction sites act as the host venue only—they just offer auction space for not-for-profit organizations to stage their own charity auctions.

Serve Yourself: Auction Site Services

Venues also differ in the services they offer to their members (and to those who just happen to click by). As you're finding the sites that cater to your buying or selling tastes, be sure to consider the different site services that are most important to your overall success.

AuctionWatch.com has more!

Don't miss AuctionWatch.com's in-depth, unbiased reviews of all the major auction sites. You'll learn which sites are the best for your online auction business.

http://www.auctionwatch.com/awdaily/reviews/index.html

Specifically, look for the following:

Inventory

Sounds like a no-brainer, but you'd be surprised at how many pretty auction sites you'll come across that are bare as the proverbial Hubbard cupboard. Here's why good inventory is so important:

- If you're looking for something truly rare or unique, go to the site with the most items up for auction—the more items up for auction, the better your chances of finding exactly what you want.

- If you're looking to sell and hope to get a decent price for your stuff, again, it's the sites with larger inventories that will bring in more potential bidders.

Site Design

Ease of use and intuitive design are key considerations among auction-goers. As one of the crowd, here's what you should be looking for:

- How easy is it for you to navigate an auction site?

- Can you find what you want quickly or do you spend a lot of time perplexed and frowning, wondering how to get to the stuff you're after?

- If you're a buyer, you'll probably lose interest in a difficult-to-use auction site.

- If you're a seller at a difficult-to-use site, your best buyers have probably already clicked on out.

Site Security

Safety and privacy are high on any Net crawler's list. Look for the following attributes:

- Every bona fide auction site should offer a thorough explanation of how members' privacy is protected.

- Sites should explain fully and clearly how users' personal information (user ID, password, credit card info, and so on) is encrypted and otherwise secured from prying eyes.

- If you're not comfortable with a site's security safeguards, don't sign up.

Site Policies and Stability

Why do stability and operating policies go hand in hand? Site policies and stability safeguards will affect your business as buyer or seller. Ask these questions of a site at which you're considering doing business:

- What is the site's policy if its server crashes—who wins an auction, is the auction extended, and what about lost bids?

- Does a site offer refunds to sellers whose auctions close during an outage?

- Does a site stick by its policies consistently or does it have too many "exceptions" and ambiguously-defined recovery protections (that don't necessarily protect *you*).

- Make sure you agree with the site's server-crash policy and customer guarantee, and also be clear about the other site policies that will affect you, such as terms of service, member responsibilities, and so on.

Customer Service

There may be times when you have questions or will need assistance. Often, you'll need to interact directly with the auction site. Therefore, consider the following points:

- Is there someone you can talk to or are you on your own when questions (or worse, troubles) arise?

- What are the hours for customer service?

- Is customer service actually staffed, or is it just a static list of FAQs and/or automated e-mail responses?

- How well-trained is the customer service staff and how quickly do they respond (in the case of e-mail support)?

- If you're dissatisfied with the customer service, who can you contact up the ladder?

- What have others said about a site's customer service? Ask around.

Special Services

More than ever, auction sites are launching additional services to catch your eye and reel you in. Consider what services are provided and how they'll be useful to you.

- How does the e-mail notification at a site work?

- Are you quickly informed (if at all) when you're outbid in an auction?

- Are there services that tell you when items you're interested in show up on the auction block?

- Are there easy-to-use screens and tools that help you keep track of all your buying and selling activities?

- Overall, how well does the site's design and operational philosophy meet your specific needs?

- Also, look at some of the high-powered services and nifty little goodies to determine if they're truly useful and efficient or if they're just brightly packaged fluff. Watch out for *feature bloat,* which occurs when special features tend to act more as hurdles than helpers to your progress.

Codes of Conduct: Auction Site Rules

Since everyone's going to have to get along, everyone needs to follow some rules. Auction rules are pretty straightforward at B2C sites: they have the stuff, they tell you how to bid, and then you pay if you win. No great controversy there. Site rules truly come into their own at the P2P venues where average citizens meet, mingle, and make deals. In these venues, where you're pretty much left on your honor, there are certain rules you'll have to abide by during your visits.

Honor Your Bids

You can't get more basic than this, and this is the core of what makes auction sites work (or fail).

- Any bid that is placed is considered a contract to purchase. It's not a game. At most sites, a winning bid is considered a binding agreement by site rules and must be honored to maintain privileges of use (though some detractors might thumb their nose at being *forced* to pay up).

- A bid should be regarded as a sincere agreement that, if successful, the stated price will be paid quickly and in full.

- Determine if the site strongly promotes bidder responsibility. If not, it's doubtful that the site will survive in the competitive auction marketplace.

Honor Your Sales

It works both ways: sales must be honored with the same regard as bids.

- Sellers must stand by the auction of their items.

- Whenever a successful high bid has been received, the seller must sell at that price (unless there is an unmet reserve price or some other previously announced condition that might render the final high bid invalid).

- If a seller backs out on a sale, the site should take action and revoke the seller's registration. (Seasoned auction-goers grumble that this sort of disciplinary action doesn't occur fast enough or often enough to offenders.)

- A site that's soft in this area isn't worth the risk.

Provide Timely Responses

Were you just notified of a winning bid? Did your item just sell? Does someone have a question? Is the check in the mail? To make online auctions successful, timely response is required of everyone involved.

- Sites will often stipulate "time windows" within which responses or next steps are to be taken.

- High bidder status might be forfeited or the honoring of a high bid might be duly dismissed if bidders and sellers aren't progressing to the completion of a deal.

- In general, timely response to e-mail questions or the closing of a deal is strongly encouraged lest you discover you've been branded as something of a risk.

No Unauthorized Use

Of anything! Sites are careful to monitor for improper behavior of their members or any attempt to use the information of other members in unauthorized ways. Namely:

- No spamming.

- No harvesting of e-mail addresses or personal contact information for unauthorized use (by the site or by the individual).

- No attempts at interfering with the proper function of the site's operation or services.

- No use of bogus user accounts for the purpose of sales fraud or any harassing activity.

No Unauthorized Items

You can't sell your little brother, nor is a spare kidney the sort of thing to plop onto the auction podium. Actually, auction sites have just about seen and hosted it all and they're usually ready to respond.

- Sites post lists of forbidden items—firearms, body parts, animals, and so on. Know what's forbidden before you list.

- Sites partner with others to prevent listing and illegal sales of infringing items (such as copyrighted materials).

- Sites will quickly shut down auctions of forbidden or infringing items.

- Many sites now follow an auction shutdown with revocation of the seller's site privileges and will also prosecute sellers to the fullest extent of the law—and that can and does mean jail time, as some sellers have already discovered the hard way.

No Manipulation

In essence, sites do not tolerate methods or schemes to manipulate bid prices or final high-bid values. That means you are warned about posting bogus bids, artificial bid "shields," or any other sort of bidding activity that could falsely raise or lower high-bid values to your gain. Sounds intriguing, doesn't it? You'll learn more about price manipulation in Chapter 6.

Of course, all auction sites will have additional rules that you'll want to carefully review before you become a member. However, those you've just read are the big hitters, the ones you need to understand thoroughly before you decide to join up at a particular site. And, beyond that, consider these two points before you proceed:

- Know the rules before you register. That's right—it's *your* responsibility to fully understand the rules of an auction site before you participate. Sites have learned over the years what can and will occur in the auction venues, and they have a hopper full of legal text that covers most eventualities. You need to decide whether those terms are agreeable to you and if they will offer the protection and peace of mind you want as you work at the auction places.

- Know what will happen if you or others break the rules. And in the case of an infraction, what course of corrective action will be taken? Will you get booted out? Will the baddie who just scammed you get booted out? Will you both get booted out regardless of whose fault it was? This is the sort of thing you'll want to understand at the beginning (but be forewarned that many site policies are difficult—some would say impossible—to fully enforce).

The Ritual of Registration

Though not truly a ritual, you might sometimes feel as if registering at some auction sites involves significant pomp and circumstance. Most auction sites require quite a bit of information before they'll turn you loose to buy or sell at will.

Name, Address, and Phone Number

Nothing surprising here. You need to be reachable via traditional methods, so you'll hand over the usual personal data.

E-mail Address

And, of course, the now common e-mail information will help the site and other users to interact with you quickly and easily.

Register at multiple auction sites at once with AW's Universal Registration service, which instantly registers you at eBay, Yahoo Auctions, Amazon.com Auctions, and more. Find it at https://secure.auctionwatch.com/ureg

Credit Card Information

Though not all sites require this information, many do. Your credit card information is used to bill you for any usage fees you incur. Also, most B2C sites will prefer to charge your credit card immediately if you win an auction, allowing them to collect payment right away and get your item on its way to you. For some auction-goers, providing credit card information up front is cause for discomfort.

Personal Profile Data

Do you currently own or rent? How did you find the site? What is your hamster's name? Some sites will ask the usual market demographic information when you register. It should be optional to answer, and you might elect to skip it. Otherwise, expect to receive notice of "special offers designed especially for you" (and your hamster, too).

For the most part, that covers the info you'll need to provide. You can expect registration to be something of a two- or three-step process: you provide initial data, the site sends an e-mail message to you to verify what you've provided, you enter a secret key code that was provided, the site then e-mails you a temporary password, and so on. The sites are good about explaining the process and what you'll need to do to complete a successful registration. Read the rules, read the site policies, and read the procedures for registering. If it's a site you like and the rules and regulations meet your approval, sign up.

Developing an Appreciation: Critiquing Online Venues

You've read already about many elements to consider when choosing an online auction site. One of your keys to personal success and satisfaction will be to learn how to effectively "grade" a site based on what you've just learned—site design, security, inventory, rules, and so on. Most auction-goers have become very astute venue critics, as will you. Consider, then, some additional factors that will help you assess whether a site measures up to your standards.

Market Prevalence

Is bigger better? You bet. Here's why:

- Most auction-goers these days are rightfully concerned with the volume of traffic that flows through a venue's portals on any given day.

- To buyers, traffic and prevalence equate to inventory and selection.

- To sellers, traffic and prevalence equate to higher numbers of potential customers.

- And to the venues, consistent levels of traffic or the lack thereof can make or break their business (and yours!).

Community

This is more relevant to the P2P sites.

- What is the overall attitude of the other folks with whom you'll regularly rub elbows?

- Has the venue clearly established (and is it upholding) an overall value system that guides all members to the best ways of doing business?

- Does the venue suffer from community indifference that could affect future traffic or inventory?

- Is there a general lack of certainty regarding the presence of good business practices and community responsibilities?

Design Stability

Not to be confused with site stability (availability), design stability concerns the overall stasis of the site's features, screens, and core usability.

- If a site is constantly changing screens, processes, or other interfaces, members will have to constantly relearn them. Most people won't want to continually slow down and retrain themselves on how to use a site.

- Although it's always good business to change with the times and offer features and amenities that are helpful and desirable, constant tinkering under the hood could indicate a venue's lack of long-term vision. If you're trying to do regular business at a site that's in constant redesign, you'll learn quickly that you're at the mercy of the landlord's whims.

Community Involvement

Many auction-goers want to be involved in the direction and decisions of their favorite auction site. Long-term members consider their efforts to be key to a site's longevity (and profitability), and feel they should be polled regarding how a site will address issues such as site improvement and problem resolution. Perhaps you'll feel the same way.

User Feedback and Site Ratings

Most sites offer some sort of forum or other means by which users can post feedback for one another or for the managers of the site itself.

- Referrals and testimonials are of highest value to everyone involved.

- Bidders are looking for others' views of how well a site works, how trustworthy sellers are, or just how "healthy" the overall community appears to be.

- Sellers are looking for feedback to determine which bidders are eager to close a good deal and which are playing the old bid-and-run game.

- Sites are eager to keep a finger on the pulse of the community, since its health is a direct reflection of how well the site is doing at creating a positive environment for business.

- Users (buyers or sellers) need to hear what other members are saying about a site in order to determine whether it's a stable environment in which to establish their business, or if it's a venue of turmoil and confusion.

AuctionWatch.com has more!

Want to know how AuctionWatch has rated different sites based on style and services? To see who makes the grade, use this link: http://www.auctionwatch.com/ awdaily/reviews/ratings.html

The "F" Word: Fees

If you think all this auction stuff happens at no cost, think again. Auction sites incur operating expenses that need to be paid for—and that's where you come in. The B2C sites don't usually charge any sort of usage fee—they're pulling down commissions from the merchants they host or making a profit from selling their own items directly. P2P sites, on the other hand, have to pay their monthly bills to keep the venue up and running, especially since they don't have merchandise they're selling directly. Therefore, they charge fees. And, though fees are usually the burden of the seller, there are times when the buyer pays a special fee, too.

Listing Fees

If you're a seller who's listing items at a venue, it's typically going to cost something to post your auction.

- From as low as 10 cents to as high as $2 (sometimes more), listing fees generate immediate income for the venue every time you put goods up for auction.

- The listing fee is usually calculated based on the minimum bid or reserve price you establish (as at eBay), but some sites have flat rate listing fees that don't change.

- Some sites don't levy listing fees at all (a tactic used to encourage more folks to list and help "grow" the site and its inventory).

- A site's fee structure is subject to change at any time, though usually a change is preceded by some forewarning.

Sales Commissions

As the name implies, these are commissions charged to the seller of an item (at the P2P or some niche sites) that are a percentage of the final high bid. You'll see this referred to as a "Final Value Fee" or "FVF" by many auction-goers. Again, it's another way the hosting venues generate income to keep the site profitable and online.

Buyer's Commissions

This was what was hinted at earlier—at many of the high-end auction sites, buyers also pay commissions on the final value of the item. This practice is a carryover from the buyer's commissions that high-end houses charge at their RL auctions.

Special Feature and Listing Fees

At some sites, special listing features will add visibility to a listing, and will also add cost to the seller. Expect to pay extra for these extras:

- Bold lettering

- "Featured Auction" or other premium placement

- Special icons

- Photo gallery placement

- Special selling price conditions (such as reserve prices)

AuctionWatch.com has more! _____

Compare the major dynamic pricing venues' listing and commission fees with AW's "Online Auction Rate Card," at http://www.auctionwatch.com/awdaily/reviews/ratecard/index.html

Keeping Up with Current (Auction) Events

As this is being written, online auctions have already established a history of their own. In regard to events, developments, shakeouts, and shake-ups, online auctions have seen so much activity that it might appear they've been around for decades (though it's only been less than one decade). So what? So how will you keep up with what's going on and what's coming up at the online venues? Just as you have a wide variety of venues from which to choose, you also have a wide variety of reporting and analysis services to help you keep abreast of the latest developments.

Auction Site Forums

Many sites host forums where members can meet and chat about the site, its members, and its direction. Good sites will have moderators that respond to member questions and comments while also posting notices of upcoming services, upgrades, or special events.

AuctionWatch.com

Of course, AW is the leader in auction advocacy and timely auction information. With regular daily and weekly news updates, special reports and features about all things auction, plus one of the Internet's most active discussion forums (the Message Center), AW works hard to keep you in touch and in tune with the online auction world.

Nasdaq.com

If you're going to put your eggs in *any* basket, find out how financially secure that basket is by keeping tabs on a site's fiscal health. Nasdaq.com tracks all the publicly traded online auction venues and provides extremely useful analyses and press releases that keep you informed on how well your chosen venues are doing in the highly competitive online marketplace.

CNET.com

If you're looking for more news and information about technology and the online world, C/NET offers it in heaping helpings. C/NET's "Top Tech News" features and special reports keep you up to date on the latest happenings. The site even hosts its own auctions—go figure.

Wired.com

More tech news you can use, with a bit more attitude thrown in for flavor.

The Mind and Mentality of the Auction-Goer

Who cares what the other folks are like, right? Wrong. If you're going after the stuff, you'll be doing so among thousands (and even millions) of other folks. If you're going after sales, you need to understand the clientele so as to serve and satisfy them. Since cyberspace is devoid of tone, inflection, and sometimes the chance to clarify your intent, it's wise to understand who's in there with you and how you can work best to keep the peace. To reach your own goals, you'll do well to understand the goals of those around you.

Casual Goers

These are your hobbyists, looky-loos, and browsers. They're here to kill a few minutes or a few hours, but they're just doing it for the fun. They might be hesitant to offer much personal information (being unsure if it's really safe) and they're probably not too interested in striking up e-mail conversations with strangers. They bid on specific items of interest and might venture into selling on occasion. They're probably not too interested in bidding wars, that is, in battling tooth-and-nail against someone else for an item. They're just here for a good time, thank you.

Hard-core Buyers and Sellers

These folks have found the auctions to be treasure troves of great stuff or untapped veins of bountiful income from which to draw. Hard-core buyers will canvass an auction site (several sites, actually) looking for specific items and will pounce—either immediately or at the very end—to win an item. Their motivation might be to acquire desirable items no matter what the cost. On the other hand, they might be interested in buying for resale, in which case they'll methodically comb the listings for "steals and deals" that allow room for profits on resale.

The hard-core sellers are making money. They've found the auctions are great places to generate extra income. They'll either offer everything under the sun (often what they bought at last week's flea market) or they'll specialize in a particular commodity. They typically know the value of their stuff if they're specialists, though they may be less than informed if they're simply turning items over quickly. Many of them dream of turning their efforts into a golden path to retirement (and some are well on their way).

Small Businesses

These folks have either made the jump from hard-core seller to bona fide business, or they've been an established business and are making the jump into cyberspace. Whichever, they're here to maximize the return on their efforts and minimize their costs. They'll work hard to run a good business, but they're not interested in dilly-dallying about or getting locked into any situations that are emotionally (as opposed to fiscally) driven. They want to please their customers, but they don't have time for nonsense. These folks are direct and to the point in their dealings—they have a business to run.

Merchants

The next step up the ladder is the merchants who typically operate with a large staff and a corporate vision. They have a process and procedure for just about everything and are usually able to provide the goods you want or the assistance you need quickly and efficiently.

Mixers and Meddlers

Seems there's always at least one creep at the playground and online auctions certainly have their share. Some folks think it's all a game, some find it a goal to challenge the status quo, and some just like to stir up the pot. Serious auction-goers don't put up with much from these troublemakers and the word has gotten out that auction sites (and even official consumer protection agencies) are ready to deal with the auctions' problem children swiftly and succinctly.

These, of course, are just rough generalizations, but they are the indicators that you'll be working with a variety of folks who all have different goals, motivations, and experiences. The best bet is to approach the auctions seriously, respectfully, but with enough lightheartedness to get along. They're all just people, so treat 'em the way you'd like to be treated.

AuctionWatch.com has more!

Want to listen in and speak up about issues and ideas that are on auction-goers' minds? Head out to the AuctionWatch.com Message Center. There's always plenty of conversation flowing. Link to it at http://www.auctionwatch.com/mesg/

Key Watch Points

- Understand the different sorts of auction sites out there (P2P, B2C, B2B) and determine which will serve your needs, either as buyer or seller.

- Be sure to understand the different auction formats, paying close attention to how the site itself defines that format—some will use familiar names but put their own spin on the rules.

- Understand which auction sites offer the services you want or need before you join up.

- Be critical of auction sites, paying special attention to their registration requirements, their site policies, and their fee structures.

- Keep current with online auction developments, both at the site and at independent sites that cover all things auction-related.

- Get a feel for the clientele before you join up. Lurk for a while, simply watching the activity, and determine whether the folks you find milling about are a crowd you can hang with.

Setting Your Sights, Establishing Your Goals

Level:	*Beginner*
Reader:	*Buyer and Seller*

Even if you don't know what you're looking for, chances are you're going to find something you want—that is, if something doesn't find you first. Strolling and browsing are all a part of online auctions, but if you're going to make the most of your efforts (and not squander hours on end), then it's good to determine *why* you're here. You don't necessarily have to have a well-defined set of goals or a corporate vision. However, when it comes to making the best use of your time, controlling your expenditures, and progressing toward whatever it is you're after, it's a good idea take a little time to chart your course so that you wind up moving in the right direction.

Knowing What You Want and Why You're Here

The immediate question is the most obvious: what are you looking for? It all depends on your goal and your reason for visiting the auction venues. Whether you're here to have fun or to cash in, knowing what you want will help you find what you desire. There are plenty of reasons why folks are turning to online auctions.

The Elusive Artifact

Previously difficult (or impossible) to find items are popping up all of the time at online auctions. For dyed-in-the-wool treasure hunters, auctions have removed many of the hurdles that once slowed (or outright prevented) finding that rare item.

- Online auctions have effectively broken down geographic barriers.

- Online auctions are accessible to anyone with a PC or other Web-enabled device and a penchant for buying or selling.

- Online auctions are the new hunting grounds for collectors, collators, and curators from all over the world.

- Online auctions regularly feature items that, in the past, might have seemed too obscure or worthless to bother selling. That's all changed now.

Find the products and deals you want quickly using AuctionWatch.com's Universal Search product, which searches hundreds of auction sites at once. Find it at http://www.auctionwatch.com/usearch/

The Killer Deal

It's the garage sale mentality. Though you probably won't be able to grab items for a mere two bits, there are still plenty of deals to be had.

- Online auctions now offer millions of items—so many, in fact that it's common to find overlooked (and therefore underpriced) items.

- With so many sites and so many items to choose from, buyers benefit from sellers' having to compete to make a sale.

- Buyers often have the new luxury of choosing from several identical items, electing to bid on the lower-priced items or bidding on several simultaneously at predetermined spending limits.

- Some sellers are eager just to unload their unwanted items and will often offer ridiculously low starting bids.

- For true bargain hunters, combing online auctions is easier, more convenient, and more productive than rummaging through boxes of junk at garage sales, thrift stores, or flea markets.

AuctionWatch.com has more!

Get the most from your online auction searches—check out AW's Performing Better Searches tip, at http://www.auctionwatch.com/awdaily/tipsandtactics/ buy-search.html

The Investment Potential

Beyond the sheer joy of finding and collecting, many folks are finding online auctions to be a key link to acquiring items for long-term gain.

- Online auctions regularly feature unique or otherwise desirable items that can be purchased inexpensively and kept until their value has appreciated.

- Often, sellers will offer very desirable items without knowing their true value or origin. The informed investor can find these items and acquire them, usually at a good (profit-bearing) price.

- Online auctions are an excellent venue when it comes time to resell a "matured" investment item—the potential population of bidders dwarfs the usual venues.

- Online auctions are an equally perfect venue for immediate turnover of items; investors can offer items recently purchased at the auctions and sell them at the same (or a different) online venue for a good (and fast) profit.

The Business Opportunity

That's what much of this is about. Online auctions are the newest way to start up or boost a business, and it's one of the safest new ventures (considering start-up investment and initial risk).

- The online marketplace is millions strong, with buyers and sellers connecting every day to exchange cash for goods or services.

- Online auctions account for billions of dollars in revenue (for the sites and their users) each year.

- Overhead investment is minimal for individuals, small businesses, or large corporations.

- With so many auction venues to choose from, buyers and sellers can reduce their expenditures and risks by being able to buy or sell in a competitive and energetic online marketplace.

- Online auctions are the hottest emerging trend in dynamic pricing, and sellers enjoy what amounts to free publicity—people drop by to see what's happening with this popular new thing, discover the seller's auction, and bid, bid, bid.

 AuctionWatch.com has more!

Have you read AW's **Starting an Auction Business** tip? Find it at http://www. auctionwatch.com/awdaily/tipsandtactics/sel-startingbiz.html

Just Browsing

The Internet was made for surfing, and many folks just want to window-shop. "No thanks, just browsing." Fair enough.

- Many auction-goers are simply entertained by a site's design and offerings.

- Many auction sites provide chat areas where members can meet and discuss trends, hobbies, or whatever.

- Online auctions are proving to be an excellent source of research where collectors, hobbyists, or other such enthusiasts can learn more about items, marketing strategies, and Internet development.

Collectors, Resellers, and Investors

We all have our reasons for buying things—utilitarian or otherwise—and they are therefore of value to us. In days past, the things we bought were to be used and then often discarded. Today, however, we have additional reasons to buy items—they may have a longer-term appeal, there may be a high present demand for them, or the thing may have potential to appreciate in value (if it hasn't already). It's these qualities that drive people to have and hold, to buy and resell, or to realize a healthy return on investment. First consider what drives the reason for purchase.

Collectors

Collectors might buy a particular item because:

- They had one (or wanted one) when they were kids and it brings back fond memories.

- They would be pleased and proud to display the item as unique decor in their home.

- They need it to fill a hole in their existing collection.

- They know the inherent value of the item though they'd never part with it for any amount of money.

- They have a passion for it and, regardless of the cost, simply must possess it.

- They just can't help themselves—it's too cool to pass up.

- They someday dream of opening their own little collectibles shop.

AuctionWatch.com has more!

Every week, AW publishes market reports on collectibles, fine arts, and antiques in its "Collector's Beat" section at http://www.auctionwatch.com/awdaily/collectors/

Resellers

Resellers might buy an item because:

- They know there is a strong demand for the item in the current market.

- They think it's the kind of merchandise that their customers will appreciate.

- They have a customer that has asked to be informed as soon as a specific item becomes available.

- They can buy it at a reasonable price and resell it at a reasonable profit.

- They speculate that it's the next craze, fad, or retro trend.

- They can move the item quickly without having to incur storage costs or tie up their money for a lengthy period of time.

Investors

Investors might buy a certain item because:

- They know the 5-, 10-, or 15-year return on investment is sizable, with little chance of depreciation. They are perfectly capable of investing in the item now and keeping it for any number of years until it "matures."

- They anticipate a quick sale at significant profit though it's only a temporary window of opportunity—they must buy and sell quickly.

- They view the item as desirable only in its ability to generate significant profit.

- They may choose to keep the item (for a while) to display it for its inherent value—and a bit of bragging rights.

- They have studied the origin and association of this item and know it's a true find.

Different Strokes for… Well, You Know

The previous section offered possible motivations for different folks to purchase certain items. But just how are these folks divergent in their pursuits?

Appreciating Items

Different groups of people have their own—often quite dissimilar—reasons for appreciating, or valuing, a particular item.

- Collectors typically appreciate an item for its appearance, romantic appeal, the memories it evokes, or the simple pleasure it provides.

- Resellers typically appreciate an item for its ability to generate another sale, to broaden their offerings, and to please customers.

- Investors typically appreciate an item for its inherent value, either as a short-term moneymaker, as a long-term asset, or as a status symbol.

Reselling Items

Likewise, different people have different views (and abilities) on parting with their possessions.

- Collectors often find it nearly impossible to part with their treasures— that is, unless they've recently purchased a finer example or are no longer interested in the collection and wish to collect something different.

- Resellers are in business to sell—they cannot afford to become emotionally attached to their merchandise.

AuctionWatch.com has more!

Learn how to buy low and sell high. See AW's tip on Buying for Resale, at http://www.auctionwatch.com/awdaily/tipsandtactics/sel-resale.html

- Investors are ready to sell the moment an item's demand is peaking or if they're in a situation where they need to liquidate some items to buy into an even more promising investment opportunity.

In Regard to Their Peers

People with different motivations for buying things naturally have different reasons to cooperate—or not—with their peers.

- Collectors often work with other collectors to help one another find things they desire.

- Resellers are friendly enough with one another and sometimes share good business practices, but they're usually resistant to offering up information that might lose them the edge over their competitors.

- Investors definitely converse with one another, but are generally disposed to build their personal wealth quietly; they sometimes remain quite private about their personal holdings.

Shared Goals, Shared Habits

On the other hand, collectors, resellers, and investors do share some common traits.

Hot Tips

- Collectors often keep good deals and hot finds to themselves, at least until they've drawn from the fountain.

- Resellers use any tip to gain advantage (though not unfairly) over their competition, and will keep such information or inventory strategies to themselves. When they go public with their edge, the competition can only strive to follow suit.

- Investors act swiftly on tips, verify potential, and make their move. They might spread the wealth or they might buy out the whole opportunity for short-term and long-term returns.

Buying Outside of a Field of Interest or Expertise

- Collectors will sometimes buy something they don't currently collect if it's something they're considering branching into (having heard that it's rare, valuable, or intrinsically interesting) or if they know they can trade it for something they *do* collect.

- Resellers will buy new and different sorts of items if they sense a trend beginning, customers continue to ask for such items, or there's otherwise an opportunity to expand their potential appeal to different customers.

- Investors stray outside their field to capitalize on additional opportunities. By doing so, they not only increase their potential for acquiring solid assets but also broaden their knowledge of different items and markets.

These are only a few of the traits of the collector, reseller, and investor that are useful to consider, even though they cannot be universally applied to any of the groups. You may relate to one, all, or none of these traits. There are no absolutes in collecting, reselling, and investing. However, there are certain behaviors and motivators that will drive each of these personalities in either different or similar directions.

Finding What You Seek

You previously learned (or have discovered on your own) that there are many auction sites online today and, when combined, offer millions of items available at any given time. With such a sea of goods, how will you find the stuff you want without spending days on end or missing out on some great offerings? Here are some ways to help you sift through the wares and home in on the things you want.

Browse: The Old Fashioned Way

It's not the most efficient approach, but there's nothing wrong with browsing the myriad listings in an auction site's catalog of item categories.

- Allow yourself plenty of time—there's plenty to look at.

- Start with the major item categories (then subcategories) that might have the sort of items you're after.

- Keep an eye open for miscategorized or misspelled items—something in the wrong category is apt to draw a smaller group of bidders, which is good news for you if you're browsing to buy. Of course, avoid such mistakes if you're preparing a listing to sell!

- Be persistent in your browsing—many items get lost in the listings and could be just the gold you're looking for, overlooked or ignored by everyone else.

- If you're of a mind to sell, pay close attention to how items are categorized and posted: did something catch your eye by the way it was categorized or did something almost slip by you for the same reason? This is what you'll want to keep in mind as you think about listing your own items someday soon.

Search

If you want to conserve time, use a site search and enter keywords for *exactly* what you're seeking.

- Use common descriptive words or names, including common misspellings.

- Often, you'll find exactly the things you're after or will quickly find out if the site has any such stuff up for auction (without time-intensive browsing).

AuctionWatch.com has more!

For even better results, take advantage of AuctionWatch's *Universal Search*. Enter your keywords and the Universal Search feature will search multiple auction sites for you and provide links to the site pages where you can bid on (and hopefully win) what you're after. You'll see the Universal Search on every AuctionWatch.com page (look at the top of the home page and in the left column of the other pages).

Featured Auctions

If someone paid good money to gain premium placement, you may as well see what all of the hubbub is about.

- Browsing featured auctions and photo-gallery auctions is much more time-manageable than scanning the *entire* listing of goods.

- You might find what you want or at least quickly find a seller who's offering the kinds of things you're searching for.

- Since featured placement often incurs higher listing fees, you're more apt to find higher-end or higher-quality items more quickly in the featured listings (their inherent value will often bear the cost of featured status).

Shopping Agents

Many auction sites and third-party sites offer shopping "bots"—you tell the bot what you're looking for and it notifies you via e-mail whenever a new item shows up that hits on your keywords.

- You can specify whether only item titles or item descriptions (or both) will be searched for keywords.

- Sites offer varying duration for their shopping bots—they might remain active for 30 days, 60 days, or indefinitely.

Linked Web Sites, Referrals, and References

Many auction sites have links and banners to other venues or establishments that might cater to your desires.

- Many sellers include links to their personal or business Web sites.

- Many merchant sites offer links to sub-brands or affiliate services.

- Some sites include links to "opt-in" mailing lists or discussion boards where you can meet more people with similar interests and businesses.

The Buddy System

It's actually called *networking* and most buyers and sellers do it.

- Establish business relationships (or just a friendly relationship) with others who sell what you're buying or are looking for similar stuff.

- The more eyes you have open for you out there, the better are your chances to locate the items you are searching for.

- Expect to return the favor for others, finding and notifying them of items you've recently spotted.

- Keep the communication flowing (e-mail, snail-mail, telephone) to keep the buddy system alive and well.

Other Resources

That's just for your online searches. Remember, online auctions and the Internet are merely the newest tools that help you reach your acquisition goals. The wise person maintains a broad pool of resources to also include all the usual (and not-so-usual) venues and vehicles. Therefore, don't forget these long-time resources and methods.

Local Dealers and Consignment Shops

Besides boosting your chances of finding the things you want, regular visits to the local shops will allow you to strike up some friendships—and add yet more eyes to your search.

- These folks can keep watch out for certain items that flow through their stores or they can keep your wants in mind when they're out on buying excursions.

- Frequently, they will let you know when an item you've been asking for has just been located or has been brought into the store for sale.

Trade Papers and Other Publications

Before the Internet and the online auctions, trade papers and market journals paired up sellers with buyers.

- Many publications are in the form of classified ads catering to specific interests.

- Much of the stuff is being sold at market prices, but just as much is being listed for quick turnover by desperate sellers who simply can't store it any longer.

- Usually, the publication will feature articles that tell more about specific sorts of items, their origins, values, and general whereabouts.

- Many dealers and show promoters advertise heavily in these publications.

Catalogs and Mailing Lists

If you've been acquiring items for any period of time, you've no doubt found out about dealers and businesses across the nation and across the world who peddle such wares. Getting on mailing lists and receiving regular catalog updates can land you an elusive item.

- Again, strike up a casual relationship with the business or individual who publishes the catalog—the more eyes, the better.

- Make your wants known—folks who publish such lists and catalogs are eager to find the things you want and generate additional sales for their businesses.

Garage Sales, Estate Sales, and Flea Markets

Some people love 'em, some abhor them, but the fact is, these venues are big business and are always hopping with pickers, peekers, and pokers. Stories have been told of renowned collectors donning unassuming attire and digging through the heaps with everyone else. Why? Great stuff is stashed away in people's simple belongings all the time. Occasionally, this stuff is unearthed and sold at barnyard prices. That's why.

AuctionWatch.com has more!

Live a day in the life of a flea market expert; check out AW's feature, "The Junker: A Day at the Flea Market," at http://www.auctionwatch.com/awdaily/features/fleamarket/index.html

Friends, Family, and Neighbors

You can't possibly attend every sales event or be at all the right places at all the right times. However, those you know and love might be able to help out and it's common for others to stumble across items for which you've previously expressed interest. Don't believe it? Next time you're at a garage sale, flea market, or wherever, look around and see how many folks are on cell phones describing an item to the person on the other end and asking how much they'd be willing to pay for it. They're out there and they're working together to find the stuff they want.

Setting Your Limits (and Sticking to Them!)

Once you've determined the things you're after, where you might find them, and how you'll go about uncovering them, you'll most likely encounter an array of items that you'd love to have or simply can't live without. Congratulations, you're a successful hunter. However, be advised that you'll find more than you can possibly afford (unless your last name is Rockefeller or Gates). When the items start turning up, it's hard to turn them down. You'll need to get control, otherwise you'll quickly spiral off into a debt-laden, account-depleted existence and probably develop a nervous tic, to boot.

Be Informed

The best way to mind your clams is to buy prudently and with sufficient knowledge.

- Whether collecting, reselling, or investing, the wise buyer knows the intricate details of every purchase.

- Do your research and you'll stand a better chance of buying *exactly* what you want instead of accidentally purchasing a knock-off, replica, or other less-than-authentic item.

- Your well-rounded knowledge of the things you buy will be crucial to understanding the value (and potential maintenance costs) of your investment.

- Knowledge and education about items helps determine what other items might be related—either from the same source, time period, or whatever. This knowledge helps you avoid purchasing additional items that are unrelated or essentially useless in helping you reach your goal.

Establish a Budget

Determine going in how much you can or will pay for an item and stick to it.

- At online auctions, a maximum bid (by way of the proxy system) is the best way to control your outlay. Place a bid within your budget and see how it fares.

- Items for which you're outbid will have exceeded your budget, so from a cost-efficiency perspective, you've lost nothing.

- Auctions you win are controlled purchases that remain at or below your predetermined bidding budget.

- Auctions you lose allow you reapply those funds to other items.

- Often, the item you lost out on—or one just like it—will show up again. You'll have the funds to bid on it the next time around.

AuctionWatch.com has more!

Learn to put your budget into practice; see AW's Bidding on a Budget tip, at http://www.auctionwatch.com/awdaily/tipsandtactics/buy-budget.html

Watch for Trends

What's hot today can be cold tomorrow (and vice versa). If you're buying, try to avoid the hype and high prices of trendy items.

- If you see the trend coming, buy before prices peak.

- If you miss buying before the trend peaks, wait until after the hype dies down and prices settle into a more affordable range (this is effective if you're buying but not if you're selling).

- And, if it is a trend, be sure you're not just buying because it's "all the rage"—chances are it will be an impulse buy that might not be as satisfying a week or month down the road.

Put the Tools to Work

Use those search tools to ferret out the specific items you're after. Browsing, aside from being very time-consuming, can also be very cash-consuming; it's easy to stumble across something you weren't looking for and quickly convince yourself you must have it or must invest in it. Purchasing on impulse might work out well for you, but chances are you'll regret it later.

Stay Focused

It's easy to be tempted by many of the things you'll see. Make a plan and stick to it.

- Develop a list of the items you're searching for and search *only* for those items.

- Once you've acquired the items you were after, make a new list for the batch of things you'd like to focus on next.

- A specific list or plan ensures that your available funds are devoted to the items you truly want, and are readily available when those items show up.

Sell, Sell, Sell

Despite your best efforts, sometimes cash can be in short supply. Don't forget one of the most obvious income-generating tools right under your nose.

- You can always sell items at the auctions to generate income for present and future purchases.

- If you have items that you're ready to part with, put 'em up for auction.

- The most efficient way of purchasing anything is with money you made from previous sales.

Look Away

Sometimes you'll need to go cold turkey. If your finances are running a bit thin, do the right thing and log off. Expect that most items have a way of showing up time and time again. Skip this crop and wait for them to come 'round the next time. Maybe then you'll be on better financial ground.

Appreciate What You Have

And one of the best ways to control your expenses is to get out of acquisition mode. To a lot of folks, buying is the goal, sometimes to the point of overshadowing the actual items purchased. If you are tossing your acquisitions on the heap, so to speak, and running off for the next great find, take a break and appreciate the things you have. You might find you've met your goals already. Wouldn't that be nice?

The Basics of Supply and Demand

Luckily, the basics are just that—basic. Though your Economics professor worked hard to impress you with facts, figures, and minutiae of the buying and selling world, the bottom-line information you need is actually very straightforward. At online auctions—or at any other venue where folks are buying and selling interesting stuff—it's sometimes a game of cat-and-mouse, of offers too good to be true and items so rare it's incredible that you're actually holding one in your hand. But is it rare, is it incredible, or is it just a bit of salesmanship? You may need some help in sorting it all out.

Demand

An item, commodity, or service must be considered desirable by many people before it can establish a generally accepted market price (one that's worth talking about, anyway). Following are a few aspects of, and influences on, demand:

- Demand can be attributed to an item's general physical appearance (it's nice to look at).

- Demand can be influenced by an item's nostalgic appeal (a *big* key to demand today).

- Demand can be influenced by an item's origin (it was fashioned by a hermit in the East Andes or was a factory misprint that was detected and corrected in subsequent runs).

- Demand can be influenced by any widespread belief in the item's potential to appreciate in value.

- Demand can be fleeting, though—hot today, iced tomorrow.

- Demand can be regional: an item can be in short supply in a particular place and plentiful in another.

- Demand can be influenced by rumors, false facts, or outright fabrications of the truth.

Supply

Pretty simple—how many are there to go around?

- Supply is typically determined (initially) by the anticipated demand for an item.

- Supply can be affected by the short production life of an item if demand does not meet initial expectations.

- Supply can be increased if demand is high enough and shows no present signs of trailing off.

- Supply of authentic goods can be augmented by reissues, repressings, and reproductions (and you'll need to be able to tell the difference).

- Supply can be artificially and temporarily controlled to manipulate the sustained demand for an item (as with Tickle Me Elmo dolls or Beanie Babies).

- Supply, like demand, can also be affected by region, copyrights, and geographic laws.

- Supply is finite: at any given point, there will be only a certain number of the items available to own regardless of whether the item is mass produced, currently out of circulation, a long-lost piece of the past, or a hand-made limited edition (plus every possible combination in between).

Demand and Supply Economics

And so it all comes down to the relationship between supply and demand—that's what determines market value. The relationship is sometimes tricky and occasionally subject to interpretation, but in a nutshell, here are the most common scenarios:

- If demand is high and supply is low, prices soar (the most obvious scenario).

- If an item is extremely scarce (perhaps one-of-a-kind), the supply might not be large enough to have developed any significant demand or even awareness. It's of virtually no value except to a very select few individuals.

- If an item has been or suddenly becomes too plentiful, it becomes commonplace and is soon disregarded by most folks. The value typically falls off steeply.

- When supply is finite yet constant—essentially the same items changing hands throughout the "ownership cycle"—the demand might also be constant, resulting in a generally accepted market price.

- Reissues and reproductions (a.k.a. "repops") can satisfy the basic desires of some individuals and can sometimes drain away some of the demand for an item. Only those who insist upon an authentic piece will be left to haggle over the original supply.

- Warehouse finds—those dusty and once forgotten cartons of vintage items—can cause a sudden spike then immediate dip in item values. Suddenly, a hard-to-find item appears in pristine condition (high demand for it and high initial price paid). When the others appear later, it becomes known that more are now in existence and the price will settle.

- Condition becomes a key factor is differentiating price among a finite supply of items. The closer to pristine condition, the more valuable the item is among its peers.

- Conversely, some items improve with aging. Furniture, wine, and historical relics often are of more value as they show signs of age and use (e.g. the development of a "patina"). Such an item in pristine condition might indicate recent cleaning or restoration, possibly diminishing the item's value and leaving fewer in their proper historic condition.

Again, these are the most common scenarios. Expect to find variations and interpretations on all these situations.

AuctionWatch.com has more! _____

The most successful sellers are ahead of the curve; See AW's tip on Buying on Speculation, at http://www.auctionwatch.com/awdaily/tipsandtactics/buy-spec.html

When to Buy (and When to Consider Selling)

Beyond supply and demand, you need to know your marketplace so as to decide when it's a good time to make your purchases. In these high-tech, nano-paced times, if you blink you just might miss your best opportunity to acquire something you've been seeking. The key, of course, is to know when the best buying and selling opportunities are about to present themselves.

Recognizing the Best Times to Buy

Everyone would like to think they can spot buried treasure from a mile away, but the truth is that many wouldn't recognize it if it bit them on the nose.

Since there are different reasons to buy, there are necessarily different definitions of the "best time to buy:"

- Buy when you can afford to. What better time is there?

- Buy when you see the item you crave. This doesn't mean to regularly buy on impulse. But keep in mind that if you merely make a mental note of where you spotted some treasure, exercising admirable control and planning to buy a little later, that treasure will most likely be discovered by someone else before you return. Collectors know to grab a rare item when they see it.

- Buy ahead of the curve. Stay tuned to coming trends, events, or celebrations (perhaps tied to world history, holidays, movie releases, award presentations, or whatever) and buy related items or investments at lower prices *before* the public hype (and subsequent demand) is high.

- Buy after the dust has settled. Hype and trends are funny in their fickleness. And with more and more of them being fueled by a hyperactive marketing, today's gold might be tomorrow's pyrite, quickly replaced by the next big thing. You can pick up your booty after the looters have dropped it in pursuit of the next treasure.

- Though it's often uncertain, you can sometimes prosper when buying the stuff that no one's paying attention to—that's true for stock, collectibles, and artwork. Sometimes, just sometimes, you might have a true sleeper on your hands that will be limited in supply when it finally takes off—and your thoughtful purchase will escalate in value very nicely.

- And, though it isn't truly a *when* scenario, buy whatever it is that you like, and buy it when you like it. Such items do have value—the personal value you assign to it.

Recognizing the Best Times to Sell

You could practically peg these times as the inverse of the best times to buy. If you buy with an intention to sell (whether right away or after some period of time) you'll want to be attuned to some of the better selling opportunities. Selling doesn't always mean you'll rake in the big bucks—that depends on your personal situation and motivation for selling—but here are some of the better times to consider liquidating your assets:

- Sell when demand is at (or near) its peak potential. This can be a gamble sometimes. If you wait too long, the wave may have passed and the spike in demand along with it.

- Sell when the bottom is about to drop out. If Beanie Babies are about to fizzle and your collection was purchased for their profit potential, then sell, sell, sell! Do it quick before the news spreads and everyone dumps theirs on the market.

- Sell when a good offer is made. It's the old "bird in the hand" thing, and the two in the bush might never materialize.

- And always sell whenever you can at least recoup or improve on your initial investment. If you've had funds tied up in stuff for a long time and need to free up some cash, sell the stuff and call it even. Remember that there was probably the value of ownership that you had enjoyed over the years, and that was worth something, wasn't it?

Understanding the Elliptical Marketplace

Does it amaze you when you see the exact same item changing hands right in front of your eyes? Not the same *sort* of item, but the *exact same piece*? Many folks tell of seeing something they once possessed making the rounds, from owner to owner, state to state, country to country. How come? The Elliptical Marketplace is in operation.

What's in the Stream

Valued goods, typically those in finite supply, are regularly traded in the resale market. Whether by a private individual or by an auction house, goods enter the "supply stream" whenever they're offered for sale, and usually on more than one occasion. Here's how it works:

- Certain commodities have inherent value and resale potential; it is what draws many folks to buy and sell them.

- Large and small collections are sold off every year at auctions (online or off) and estate sales, often causing the original collection to be fragmented among multiple buyers.

- The buyer may choose to sell at a point when a profit can be realized or there's some other reason to let go of the item; it then goes back into the supply chain.

- A new buyer spots the item and "pulls" it out of the stream.

- When the buyer decides to put the item back into the stream, the cycle repeats itself, time and time again.

So Why Is It Elliptical?

The ellipse is oval, right? That means it has a length that exceeds its height. Put your finger in the center of the ellipse and you'll notice the two points of the oval that are farther away from the center than the two sides. Sounds unrelated at first but here's how the analogy applies:

- At two distinct points, supply in the stream is farthest away from the buyer.

- When at those points, such supply seems nonexistent, hard to find, and incredibly rare. Do any still exist?

- The stream is usually in steady motion as people sell their possessions (for whatever reason).

- The sale, if at a significant price, can arouse the attention of other people who own the same or similar items—that could prompt them to sell their items.

- If demand supports it, all such items could be wrested from the woodwork and put into the stream, vastly increasing the previous limited (or seemingly nonexistent) supply.

- Now there are several to choose from and buyers are poised to make their purchases (this is analogous to the sides of the ellipse that are closest to the buyer).

- If the supply is depleted and the buyers choose to hold their purchases for a period of time, the supply is again at the farthest points of the ellipse . . . until the next wave of trading takes place.

This elliptical marketplace isn't a true economic science and it's doubtful whether you can look it up in a college textbook—it's based on experiences and observations of the resale market. But it is real and the point is to understand that when there is a drought, it's apt to be a temporary situation. As a buyer, it's necessary to keep this in mind as you choose the time you'll buy. If prices are incredibly high and you know that more such items are still out there (somewhere), bide your time and watch the market. A high-priced sale might be just the dislodged stone that brings down an avalanche of supply. *That's* when you can take your pick among the offerings.

Your Personal Power at the Auction Places

Well, by now you've seen some of the most common scenarios and situations in the buying market. And with so many options available to you, that translates to purchasing power that is no longer limited by the funds you can commit.

- The advent of the Internet and online auctions has made it easier to buy and sell goods than ever before. That offers more choice, selection, and leverage for you as a buyer.

- With selection comes competition as sellers work harder for your money, now understanding that you have the power to say no to one seller and yes to another who is offering the same item (or a better or cheaper one).

- The activity of buying and selling is wonderfully documented in auction sales. Buyers can analyze selling trends and can track the rise and fall of item demand. This lets buyers compare prices and overall shifts in accepted market value, allowing them to choose the best time to make their purchases.

- And with a worldwide marketplace filling the supply stream, bringing home the hard-to-find just got a whole lot easier.

Key Watch Points

- Have a clear understanding of what you hope to acquire or achieve at an online auction site and you'll be in a better position to choose the site that will best meet your needs.

- Will you be a collector, reseller, or investor? Many folks are one, two, or all three at the same time. Understand your motivation for buying items and be sure the item will live up to your buying expectations.

- Be choosy about the auction sites you frequent. Have a clear understanding of each site's rules, policies, and design philosophies to be sure the site will not hinder your success.

- Set a budget for your spending and stick to it.

- Understand the basic tenets of supply and demand—and their combined effect on prices. Use that knowledge to better guide you in your decisions regarding when to buy and when to sell.

- Watch the online auction marketplace: it's an elliptical stream of goods and you'll want to anticipate the cycle and buy when hard-to-find items are coming out of the woodwork—and sell when yours will look like the only one left in a barren world.

- Remember that *you* are in control. Online auctions have leveled the playing field for buyers and sellers, providing better opportunity for all to buy and sell in the open marketplace.

> **Level:** **Beginner to Intermediate**
>
> **Reader:** **Buyer and Seller**

I t's really all about this: people trading with people. Someone must be selling and someone must be buying before a transaction can take place. Though you might believe good business is based on the best merchandise, the best quality, or the best prices, the key to lasting business success comes down to personal interactions. Call it customer service, call it negotiating the deal, call it whatever you like, but it comes down to engaging in a transaction. Whether at P2P or B2C sites, you will inevitably get involved with people. In this aspect of the auction business, *how* you get involved will set the stage for your transactions every time.

Asking the Right Questions in the Right Way at the Right Time

There's no such thing as a stupid question, right? Right, but there are some questions that are less appropriate or less timely than others. To establish yourself as an informed and responsible buyer, you'll want to consider some of the best ways to get answers to your questions—getting the information you need while ensuring your queries don't cast a shadow on a potential transaction.

What Are the Right Questions?

The right questions are those that haven't been clearly answered even after you've carefully reviewed an auction description. This is key: don't ask a question that has already been answered in the seller's listing (that wastes their time and makes you look like an amateur). But if the listing is ambiguous, here are some things you'll want to ask about:

- Clarify the condition of an item. Get the most accurate description of its "grading" and, if important, ask if it's been restored or altered in any way.

- Ask if images are available if none are included in the listing (it's usually OK to ask for additional images, within reason).

- Ask about the item's provenance or documented history of ownership. Without going overboard, ask *where* the seller got it, *how long* the seller has owned it, and so on. Ask these questions only if the information is critical to determining the origin, authenticity, and value of an item.

- Clarify the seller's sales policy. Find out what shipping methods the seller uses (and at what cost), whether items are insured or tracked, and if there will be return privileges.

- Ask about a seller's history at the auctions. If someone is new to a site, politely ask if they're part of a business, if they're a private collector, and so on; but stop short of prying.

- Ask about any questionable comments in the seller's feedback rating. This is touchy stuff, but it also offers the seller an opportunity to explain why someone else decided to leave a negative comment.

AuctionWatch.com has more!

Read more tips on contacting sellers during and after an auction in AW's Contacting Sellers tip, at http://www.auctionwatch.com/awdaily/tipsandtactics/buy-contact.html

What Are the Right Ways to Ask?

Tone is everything when two people engage in discussion. However, tone is glaringly absent online. Choose your words wisely and pose your questions carefully to avoid being misunderstood.

- Never criticize a seller's listing when asking a question.

- Never try to dicker a seller down during an initial contact and especially not while an auction is in progress.

- Be clear and concise when asking your question. A shorter, more direct question will probably get a quicker, more helpful answer.

- If you have several questions, ask them in a single message. Don't dump an endless laundry list of questions, but also avoid bombarding the seller with multiple messages posing question after question.

- Be respectful and polite at all times. Never flaunt your knowledge, beliefs, or biases in a manner that could be construed as offensive or combative.

- Use e-mail—that's the preferred method to pose your questions. Though many sites offer the info, avoid contacting seller using a street address or telephone number.

What Are the Right Times to Ask?

Timing is critical for both parties. Questions need to be posed at the proper times to make the potential transaction easier.

- Always ask your questions *before* you bid.

- Ask questions while there is still enough time for the seller to respond. Don't corner someone into answering within the last few hours before the auction ends (though some sellers can respond that quickly—consider it a bonus).

- Only ask a question if you're seriously considering bidding on an item. Don't waste a seller's time with "not interested in buying, just curious" sorts of queries.

- If you want to know more about an item but you aren't interested in buying, ask after the auction, be polite and concise, and know that the seller isn't required to provide a response.

What Else Should You Know?

Your initial goal is to gain a clearer understanding of an auction item. However, as you pose your prudent questions, be aware of these little nuances in the responses you'll receive.

- How quickly did the seller respond? This could indicate how organized and committed someone is to managing successful auction transactions. If they responded slowly (or not at all), does that indicate how they'll approach the shipping of an item?

- How clear was the seller in answering your question? If there was any hemming and hawing or other evasion of your question, that could be a signal that all is not well.

- How friendly is the seller? Though lasting personal relationships aren't the goal here, a friendly seller will usually be more customer-oriented and committed to your satisfaction.

Responding to Customer Queries

Okay. The buyer's been duly schooled on how to best contact a seller. Sellers, now you'll need to step up to the line to complete the handshake. How you respond to your customers (and potential customers) will usually determine how successful you'll be in the long run.

Your Response Sets the Tone

Besides looking for answers, potential bidders are checking you out. Be sharp, be accessible, be professional, and be responsive.

- While your auctions are running, you're on duty. Check your e-mail regularly (at least once a day).

- Respond right away. Time management gurus proclaim the best way to keep up on tasks is to handle them the minute they come across your desk. In the case of questions, respond immediately upon receiving them—there could be a high-bidding customer on the other end.

- Respond clearly and concisely. Answer the questions that were asked or ask for clarification if the question was ambiguous.

- Expect multiple messages from the same bidder. Remember, someone who's asking questions is interested in your auctions. Continue to help them (within reason) and you'll help yourself to better business.

- Be professional at all times. Adopt a matter-of-fact tone in all of your correspondence. Don't be too mechanical, but make use of a tone that will never be construed as pushy or patronizing.

Your Response Sets the Pace

How and when you respond to bidder questions can subtly establish how efficiently a transaction will progress. Bidders are looking for a few good sellers who have the markings of no-nonsense businesspeople.

- Respond quickly and bidders will know you're on top of your business. Drag your feet or offer up excuses and your customers might not take you or your auction seriously.

- Respond quickly and bidders will feel the need to follow through in like manner, especially if they win and will be sending payment.

- Respond quickly and bidders will feel more at ease that you are professional and can be trusted to ship items quickly and will respond to any post-auction correspondence in the same way.

Your Response Seals the Deal

Remember, sometimes bidders who ask questions are testing the water. Your responses will beckon to them, "Come on in, the water's fine!"

- Respond thoughtfully and completely to bidders' questions and they'll feel more confident about placing a bid on your item.

- Respond to multiple queries and bidders will know you're interested in their satisfaction and not just looking for a quick buck with a chilly "all sales are final" attitude.

- Respond dutifully in all aspects of the auction and bidders will come back to your auctions again and again.

AuctionWatch.com has more!

Read more about e-mail etiquette in AW's Wording Auction Emails and Sending End-of-Auction Emails tips at

http://www.auctionwatch.com/awdaily/tipsandtactics/sel-email.html

http://www.auctionwatch.com/awdaily/tipsandtactics/sel-eoa.html

Providing Additional Information

Again for the sellers, when those questions, queries, and comments come in, a simple answer will always suffice. But, if you want to *exceed* the potential customers' expectations—and why wouldn't you?—then offer up a bit more information that might help them feel better about your auction, about your methods, and about you.

Help Your Customers Become More Informed

A question about your auction might actually be an effort by the bidder to better understand the style of items you deal in. Give them more information when you sense their desire to learn.

- Take a moment to point out distinctive features of your item and explain to the bidder why those features are important (maybe as a key to authenticity).

- Explain related items for which the bidder might also want to be on the lookout. Whether it's additional items you have up for auction or additional items that can help the bidder reach a goal (building a complete collection, for example), offer this sort of information at every opportunity.

- Provide short, interesting stories to a bidder about how you happened to own the item, why you're auctioning it, or anything else that gives them a better sense for the item's origin and your motivations for selling it.

Help Your Customers Ask Better Questions

Some bidders who work hard to ask very pointed questions often overlook the most obvious elements.

- Take the time to clarify the facts about the items you're selling, and quickly dispel any common misconceptions of which the bidder might not be aware.

- When appropriate, explain some of the investment potential in the sort of item you're auctioning. Quote other auctions or reliable sources that bidders can evaluate for themselves.

- If the bidder is overlooking an obvious question, tell them so (respectfully) and explain why most folks, especially those new to purchasing this sort of item, fail to ask the question.

- Direct your bidders to additional resources. If you have a Web site that catalogues the history of this sort of item, let 'em know. If you have a favorite Web site or book or institution that has been instrumental in developing your expertise, pass that along to your bidder as well.

Encourage the Bid

Though carnival barkers need not apply, there is justification in the legitimate business world for well-placed salesmanship. Want to get bidders off the fence and into your auction? Some of your best opportunities are during engagement.

Clear and Complete Listings

Though the details of this will be covered in Chapter 7, "Representing Yourself Like a Pro: Listing Effectively," make a mental note now that high-quality listings will immediately communicate your professional and informed style of doing business.

Accessibility

Again, keep up on your e-mail, replying quickly and completely to all messages, and bidders will feel confident that you're the seller they can reach and trust.

Extra Information

Give 'em a bit more than they asked for and they'll know you're committed to informed and truthful transactions.

Extra Effort

Help the bidders learn more about your item or similar items. Help them understand your sales methods and policies (including why you operate the way you do). Help them understand more about your business and the additional services you might provide, and they'll see you're in this not only for your benefit but for theirs as well.

 **AuctionWatch.com has more!** _____

Read more about attracting bidders in AW's Encouraging Bids tip, at http://www.auctionwatch.com/awdaily/tipsandtactics/sel-encouragingbids.html

Keys to a Smooth Transaction

Hopefully you've realized that everything discussed up to this point serves as an element to ensure a better exchange. Though you might find most of it to be well within the realm of common sense, you'll also know that common sense is frequently nowhere to be found when deals are made. Use these basic keys of good dealing to make a sale come off as smoothly as possible. Even if a sale doesn't occur, using good methods and good sense will keep you in good practice and good stead with others with whom you come in contact. There's a lot of "good" in that, huh?

- Be clear about your goals in every deal. Know why you are buying or selling. Be sure your expectations are reasonable and well founded. This clear-minded approach makes working a deal easier since your boundaries are already set.

- Keep it professional. If you don't agree with so-and-so's way of doing business, don't do business with him or her. Keep your standards high and your nose clean. If you sense a situation where you feel even a bit uneasy, take the next exit and get out.

- Be pleasant. Professionalism doesn't mean frigidity. If you come off as too businesslike, you can quickly undermine your own efforts. Be engaging, be nice, and then be sure to keep focused on the deal at hand.

- Show respect. All buyers and sellers bring their unique knowledge, style, and experience to the party. Respect people's passions, apprehensions, and motivations. The respect you show will usually be returned many times over. It's the old Golden Rule: "Do unto others as you would have them do unto you." It might sound corny, but it still applies.

- Keep an open mind. Listen to the other person and determine what they're looking to achieve. You might learn more about the folks you deal with if you lend an ear to their needs. You'll also learn more about yourself by stepping into their shoes and finding out how *your* actions and attitudes might be helping or hurting matters.

- If there's a problem, work it out. Unless you're dealing with a king mixer who just loves to stir up trouble for sport, you'll find that the other party is as eager to sort out a problem quickly and painlessly as you are. Recall stated policies and understandings (you did clarify all of that up front, right?) and use those to help untangle any snags that may have come about.

- Don't make it personal. That's sometimes the hardest thing to do, especially when it's personal interactions that are being discussed. Still, apply your professional style, your values and goals, and determine if, from a business perspective, this will be a beneficial transaction. If the hassle factor is high, cut it loose before you get in danger of having your emotions intervene.

- Welcome new friendships. Remember, we're talking about the Internet here. The Net has been founded on open communication and information sharing among millions of people from all walks of life. Expect to make friends and expect to be a friend.

The Difficult Buyer or Seller

And then the cloud moves over. Nobody wants to admit it, but with some folks it just takes more effort to keep the peace while working the deal. This doesn't mean that there are a lot of stinkers out there, but some folks do require a bit more maintenance than others.

Dealing with the Difficult Buyer

A difficult buyer might not necessarily be the high bidder (yet). They could be an interested party who seems to want much of your attention before they've bid. Then again, they *could* be the high bidder and they want their item now, now, now! Whatever the case, adopt these tactics to take control and avert a clash.

- Be sure your sales policies are clearly stated in your listings. Refer anxious bidders to those policies if there are any questions.

- Communicate clearly and consistently. Whether the bidder wants to know how they are to pay, how you'll ship, and where their item is right now, keep them posted every step of the way if they have become your customer.

- Stick to your policies. Though you want to be flexible when the need warrants, some bidders will try to push you to your limits. Calmly redirect them to your policies or succinctly restate exactly how you intend to conduct business.

- Ask point-blank what the bidder's concern is. Some have trouble expressing what's really on their mind. If they have a legitimate concern, you can quickly address it and reassure them about how you do business.

- Don't be afraid to be firm. Though still professional, you may need to diplomatically let the bidder know when to cease contacting you. You have a business to run and don't have time for endless correspondence; explain that in no uncertain terms.

- Always stay within the rules and philosophy of the hosting auction site. If you work professionally and within the framework the site has laid out, you're in virtually no danger of being accused of behaving improperly.

AuctionWatch.com has more! _____

For more on this topic, read AW's Dealing with Difficult Buyers tip, at http:// www.auctionwatch.com/awdaily/tipsandtactics/sel-difficult.html

Dealing with the Difficult Seller

The goods are there, but will the seller be good when it comes time to cut the deal? Sometimes sellers might not be as dedicated to customer satisfaction as you'd hope. Your best defense will be a good offense (without being offensive).

- Evaluate the seller based on listing style, stated policies, responsiveness to questions, and feedback posted by previous customers. Always research a seller *before* you bid.

- If you've won an auction but haven't heard from the seller, make the first move and send an e-mail message of your own. You're well within your rights to do so, provided you've given the seller 24 to 72 hours to contact you first.

- If the seller seems absent-minded or disturbingly nonchalant about closing the deal, get a clear understanding about when you'll pay, how you'll pay, and when and how your item will be shipped to you. This is a good time to consider credit card payment (perhaps using an online payment service), where you can dispute the charge if the seller doesn't come through.

- Keep in contact with the seller. Steady communication is often enough to goad a seller into action—if nothing else, to get you your item and be rid of you.

- Keep all correspondence until the deal is over, then keep it just a bit longer in case the transaction comes back in some way to haunt you (though it rarely does).

- Make a note of slack sellers and avoid them in the future.

 AuctionWatch.com has more! _____

For more on this topic, read AW's Dealing with Deadbeat Sellers tip, at http://www.auctionwatch.com/awdaily/tipsandtactics/buy-deadbeat.html

Dealing with Deadbeat Bidders

They won't pay, but you don't have to put up with it. For whatever reason, some bidders just never follow through on their agreement to buy. Understand some of the motivations for deadbeat bidding, then understand how you can combat it.

What Drives a Deadbeat Bidder?

Understanding your opponent is the first step in protecting yourself.

- Some bidders fail to recognize that online auctions *aren't* a game; they think it's fun to bid, but never intend to really pay.

- Some bidders like to challenge the online rules and will dare you to try to make 'em pay.

- Some bidders are working a scam and deadbeat bidding is a tactic to interfere in auctions (refer to Chapter 6, "Fraud: The Sale That Went South").

- Some bidders bid beyond their means and will try to avoid paying when they realize they've overextended themselves.

- Some bidders simply forget, that's all.

How Can You Respond to a Deadbeat Bidder?

You've waited and waited and still no payment. Time to take action.

- Send notice of payment due. Often, if a bidder has overlooked payment, this is all the prodding that is needed.

- Send a second notice of overdue payment and indicate that the item will be offered to the next highest bidder or relisted if the bidder doesn't pay.

- A third notice is a third strike: the bidder will lose claim to the item, will be given a negative feedback comment, and will be reported to the auction site for failure to pay. *Never use threatening or personally demeaning language here, no matter how irritated you are.*

- Keep all correspondence you've sent and any you might have received from the deadbeat bidder; you'll need it if and when an auction site investigates your complaint.

- Make note of deadbeat bidders and screen them from future auctions you post. Some sites, like Yahoo Auctions, have the equivalent of a "blacklist" where unwelcome bidders can be noted and effectively blocked automatically.

- Contact the host site and request a refund of any fees that were charged to you, explaining that the bidder never followed through. This also reasserts the reporting of a deadbeat.

- Relist the item if you wish, or contact the second-highest bidder to see if they're interested in buying at their high bid price. They're not obligated in any way, but many will jump at the deal when contacted in these situations.

How Can You Avoid Deadbeat Bidders?

It's a hassle when the deadbeats come visiting your auctions. Here are a few steps to weed them out before they infest your auction spot.

- In your sales policy, make it clear when payment is to be received. Ten days from the auction's end is the usual grace period. After that, ownership rights have been rescinded.

- Monitor the bidding on your auctions and note bidders with low or possibly negative feedback ratings. You can reserve the right to cancel anyone's bid during the course of your auction, especially the deadbeat bidder whose feedback indicates a history of this sort of activity.

- Post neutral or negative feedback about deadbeat bidders. You'll want to alert the rest of the auction community to the bad behavior; hopefully others will have done the same.

- Use site blocking tools whenever available to eliminate deadbeat bidders' involvement in your auctions.

The biggest gripe among auction-goers is the lack of action that sites take in barring deadbeat bidders. Though they may try to help, auction sites are often too lenient when it comes to bad auction behavior. At the same time, some sellers are ready to burn a bidder at the stake for the slightest infraction. Therefore, ultimate responsibility for monitoring and managing your auctions rests squarely with you.

 AuctionWatch.com has more! _____

For more on this topic, read AW's Dealing with Deadbeat Bidders tip, at http://www.auctionwatch.com/awdaily/tipsandtactics/sel-deadbeat.html

Compassion Has Its Place

Okay. With the harsh stuff having been said, is there ever a time to lighten up? Absolutely. It's easy to get worked up over simple misunderstandings and missteps, but keep in mind that these are just people dealing with people. Sometimes, things don't go as planned or as hoped. Unless you've been seriously wronged, consider letting some things slide. Ask yourself if getting upset or standing on principle is going to solve anything or result in any real gain. Remember that most people at the auctions have regular jobs and are dealing with the unexpected events of life just as you are.

- If a buyer confesses to being short on funds, consider giving them extra time to pay (within reason) and ask if they can offer a "good faith" down payment.

- If a buyer has made a mistake and bid on the wrong item, inquire what it was they were truly hoping to find. Maybe you have the thing they really want. Otherwise, if the buyer seems sincere, let 'em off the hook.

- Sometimes you'll need to bite your tongue, especially if a buyer has stood you up without much remorse. Be big about it, offer a bit of friendly advice about the need to bid carefully, and say goodbye. You could attempt to ask for reimbursement of your auction fees, but don't hold your breath; it's best to take this up with the hosting site and request a "non-paying bidder" refund.

- If it's a seller that goofed, you've only lost some time bidding on their item, provided you haven't sent money. Don't put up a stink, but try to understand why the item isn't available to you.

- If you have sent money to a seller who has slipped up, get moving and get your money back. For honest mistakes, honest sellers will typically apologize profusely and quickly return your money.

Use your own judgment in these situations and work with others in the auction community to smooth out potential bumps in the road. Sounds sugary, but it sure makes online life a whole lot easier.

Key Watch Points

- It's a world of people meeting people, even online. But it's a faceless land-scape, so take extra care in how you communicate with one another.

- Don't be bashful about asking questions of sellers or buyers—you want to be sure you can bid with confidence or sell with success.

- Be responsive to the very best of your abilities. You'll be setting the stage for an eventual transaction as well as for many future transactions.

- Offer potential bidders the information they need, then offer a bit more if it helps them feel more at ease with you and your items.

- If a deal seems to be going south, stay in communication to salvage the situation or to determine if it's better to start over with someone else.

- Be professional, polite, and pleasant in all of your interactions.

- Don't be afraid to take a stand against deadbeat bidders or lazy sellers. Make auction sites aware of any misdealings you encounter.

- Have a heart. Sometimes things just don't go well, despite everyone's best intentions.

CHAPTER 4

Policy Making— How Will You Conduct Business?

Level:	**Beginner to Intermediate**
Reader:	**Buyer and Seller**

Rules, regulations, policies, and procedures: they're what give life its direction, define its boundaries, and set everyone's expectations. You'll never know if you're playing fair unless you've first read and understood the rules. You'll never know if your rules are within reason unless you've understood what's acceptable on the playing field.

At online auctions, policies are what drive expectations among buyers and sellers. They're often referred to as *Terms of Service* (TOS), and they're the communicated agreement between a seller and the bidders and buyers attracted to an auction. What's to be specified, though? What are the most important considerations to cover? What is reasonable to expect? How do you know your TOS won't end up DOA, and how can you interpret the other sellers' TOS to ensure you won't be left SOL (*Sad* and Out of Luck)?

Auction policies or TOS—call them whatever you like, but be sure you're clear about them before you proceed. Clarity is key in the auction business—not much good comes from online misunderstandings.

The Fine Print: Read It, Know It, Live It

To start, you'll need to abide by others' TOS conditions when you're shopping, bidding, and buying at online auctions. Expect that you'll encounter many different types of policies during your travels. Not only do the sites themselves have specific *User Agreements*, their affiliates (such as payment services) will also have terms and conditions with which you must comply if you want to engage in any transaction with them or with their assistance. Of most importance to you, however, will be individual sellers' policies. They'll come in varying flavors: some are quite simplistic, while others are full-fledged dissertations and declarations. Regardless, before bidding on anyone's auction, be sure you understand the most basic conditions.

Payment

First, find out how and when buyers are asked (required?) to pay and if there are any restrictions to how payment may be remitted.

- What forms of payment are accepted (money order, personal check, credit card, online payment transaction)?

- Do you have flexibility in how you pay, or has the seller specified something like "money orders only"?

- Do you feel comfortable that your payment will be safely guarded and received? What are your chances of retrieving it if there's a problem? This is a definite concern for big-ticket purchases.

- Has the seller specified a window of time in which payment must be received, such as "payment due within 14 days of auction close"?

Shipping Costs

It's customary that buyers pay postage costs, but what will those costs be and which delivery service will be used?

- Does the seller quote a fixed postage cost or merely state "buyer pays postage"?

- Will the seller ship using only one method (carrier) and, if so, is that the most cost-effective option?

- Do you have a choice of carrier for special situations, such as shipping to a P.O. box?

- Does the seller ship internationally?

- Is the buyer required to pay "handling and supplies fees?" What are those fees?

- If shipping fees seem a bit high, is there an explanation why?

- Does the seller offer reimbursement for postage overpayment or overcharging? This can be a real bone of contention for some buyers and sellers.

 AuctionWatch.com has more!

For more on this topic, see AW's Avoiding Excessive Shipping Costs tip, at http://www.auctionwatch.com/awdaily/tipsandtactics/buy-avoidshipping.html

Insurance and Tracking

Package insurance and tracking add additional costs to shipping, costs that buyers will often agree to pay.

- Does the seller offer any insurance or tracking services?

- Is insurance and tracking an option (can you elect to forgo them)?

- Will the seller provide a valid tracking number, one that you can monitor online at a carrier's Web site?

Guarantees, Refunds, or Exchanges

And if something goes wrong or doesn't fulfill expectations (or promises), will you have recourse?

AuctionWatch.com has more! _____

For more on this topic, see AW's Identifying Questionable Auctions tip, at http://www.auctionwatch.com/awdaily/tipsandtactics/buy-identify.html

- Does the seller offer return privileges or is the item being sold "as is"?

- Has the seller stipulated return and refund conditions? (Such as "refunds only offered within 7 days of item delivery" or "all returns subject to inspection.")

- In the case of a return and refund, will you be charged any sort of "re-stocking fee"?

- How quickly will a refund be processed?

- Can you simply exchange for another item?

It's critical that you fully understand these and any other terms or conditions that a seller has stated. If any term seems unclear or hasn't been stated, ask questions to be sure you and the seller are in agreement. You're not necessarily looking for trouble by doing this; actually, you're working together to *avoid* trouble. However, if the stated policies don't sit well with you, pass the auction (and seller) by and look elsewhere; it's typically fruitless to challenge a seller's policies.

AuctionWatch.com has more! _____

Curious about your online payment, shipment, and insurance options? Check out Auction Manager's Auction Toolkit, which connects buyers and sellers with the most prominent online payment, shipment, and insurance providers, including escrow.com, iShip, ProPay.com, stamps.com, Tradesafe.com, U-Pic.com, and X.com. Find it at http://wsacp.auctionwatch.com/login.html?ret=%2Fmy%2Facp%2F

Establishing Your Sales Policy

And then the time comes when a buyer will want to understand *your* sales policy. Be sure your policy covers the key points made in the preceding section. But before you get to the nitty-gritty of deciding what payment types you'll accept or what carrier you'll use, be sure your policy is built on a firm foundation that takes the following matters into account:

- Be exhaustive but not exhausting. A clear policy that defines all of your terms is essential, but many sellers have truly gone overboard to the point that a buyer feels uncomfortable about having to agree to so many conditions.

- Be direct but not dictatorial. Most buyers appreciate clearly stated conditions, but as customers, they're also looking for some acknowledgment that their business is important to you. If your terms come off as too rigid, it might drive customers away.

- Don't be tone-deaf. "These are my terms and that's final." Sure, you're the seller and you've got the goods, but no one wants to feel they're being shoved around while doing business with you. Standing firm can be accomplished without resorting to an arms-folded, jaw-set, don't-cross-this-line stance.

- Be customer-oriented. Your goal with any policy is not only to establish your business practices but also to establish a reasonable and friendly demeanor in which you'll do business. Your policy should read as protection not only for yourself but also for your customers, too. Customer satisfaction, even in the P2P sector, is becoming a key differentiator these days in the highly competitive online auction marketplace.

- Keep up with the times. With new developments being made in areas of shipping services, payment services, and others, it's important to keep current. To you, this means investigating the latest services that seem to have gained public favor. Don't tell a customer, "No, I don't use online payment services." This might communicate that you aren't working to keep up to date or that you don't care to. To some customers, it's all they need to hear that tells them they'll be better off bidding elsewhere.

AuctionWatch.com has more!

For more on this topic, See AW's Creating a Sales Policy tip, at http://www.auctionwatch.com/awdaily/tipsandtactics/sel-salespolicy.html

Payment Methods and Services

So, now to the nuts and bolts. Payment is where to apply most of your attention; it's the money that usually makes folks nervous. Today, though, payment is becoming easier, safer, and more convenient for buyers and sellers alike. Take a look at all of the methods available, though, to be sure you're able to meet the majority of your customers' needs. There's no right answer when deciding which payment methods to accept, but take a look at the pros and cons of each in order to help you determine which will carry the greatest payoff for you and your customers.

Money Orders and Cashier's Checks

These are probably the most widely used payment tools around, largely since they've been around for so long.

Seller's Point of View

Following are the pros and cons of using money orders and cashier's checks for payment according to most sellers:

- **Pro**: They are as good as cash because they are backed by cash.
- **Pro**: They are difficult (almost impossible) to forge.
- **Pro**: They can be deposited in practically any financial institution.
- **Pro**: Some can be converted immediately to cash at certain institutions.
- **Pro**: Since they are as good as cash, sellers can ship items immediately and complete the transaction sooner.
- **Con**: Since they must be purchased from a third-party issuer, it might take a bit longer before the buyer sends the money.

Sellers still generally consider money orders and cashier's checks preferable to other forms of payment. When you include them in your payment policy, be sure to keep these points in mind:

- Encourage payment of this type, but never insist on it.

- Inform buyers that this sort of payment type earns immediate shipment of items (and be sure you keep that promise).

- Be flexible about accepting other payment types, especially when a low-cost item doesn't warrant the additional outlay for a money order or cashier's check.

Buyer's Point of View

Buyers are sometimes split when it comes to the pros and cons of these payment methods. Here's why:

- **Pro**: These payments usually ensure immediate shipment of an item (depending on the seller's service level, of course).

- **Pro**: These payments are traceable because of the unique payment number on both the payment check and the accompanying stub.

- **Pro**: Issuers will assist purchasers in certain instances if the payments are lost, stolen, or otherwise misappropriated.

- **Con**: They cost money—a money order usually carries an issuance cost between $1 and $3. Cashier's checks often cost $3 and up (sometimes determined by the face value of the check).

- **Con**: They take time—purchasers have to visit an institution that issues them.

- **Con**: Money orders usually have a maximum issuance value, so it may take more than one to cover a big purchase. Cashier's checks don't typically have this limitation, though.

Personal Checks

Personal checks are used largely out of convenience. But at online auctions, they're not always the most wanted form of remittance.

Seller's Point of View

Here's how the sellers rate personal checks as a method of payment:

- **Pro**: Payment by personal check is typically sent quickly since it is so convenient for the buyer.

- **Pro**: Sellers are able to hold shipment of an item until a personal check payment clears their bank; buyers should expect this holding period.

- **Con**: Some checks bounce. Is there any more to say?

- **Con**: A returned check will result in a returned check charge that will be assessed to the seller. The seller now has to try to get the buyer to provide reimbursement (plus an explanation).

- **Con**: Holding a check for clearing also means holding an auction transaction open for a week or two longer than would be needed for a more secure form of payment.

Personal checks do bring a bit of risk to the transaction, but 95 percent of the time they work just fine. It's reasonable to add personal checks to your payment policy, with the following provisions:

- Specify clearly that you will have to wait a prescribed period of time (usually 7 to 10 business days) until the check clears your bank before you ship the merchandise.

- Specify that buyers will be liable for any returned check charges.

- Don't discourage personal checks, even though they bring a bit of uncertainty to the transaction; rather, promote the benefits of using other forms of payment instead (for example, you ship immediately when someone pays with a money order or cashier's check).

AuctionWatch.com has more! _____

For more on this topic, see AW's Addressing Bounced Checks tip, at http://www.auctionwatch.com/awdaily/tipsandtactics/sel-bounce.html

Buyer's Point of View

For buyers, personal checks carry pretty much the same pluses and minuses as they do for sellers.

- **Pro**: Personal checks are easy and usually right at hand.

- **Pro**: Personal checks offer more budgetary control for the buyer, making it easier to monitor auction-related outflow as compared to other living expenses.

- **Pro**: Personal checks can be controlled to a degree—a check can have a stop put on it if trouble arises before the check is cashed.

- **Con**: Buyers have to wait for the check to clear before a seller ships the item.

- **Con**: An unbalanced or poorly balanced checking account can result in a bounced check. ("I can't be out of money—I still have checks.")

- **Con**: Buyers are requested to (and should) pay for returned check charges.

Credit Cards

If you're gonna run with the big successes, you'll need to be able to process credit card payments. Start by considering the traditional credit card payment: someone has a credit card and provides the card number and expiration date to the seller for payment processing.

Seller's Point of View

Using the scenario above, here are the ups and downs from where the seller is standing:

- **Pro**: Buyer profiling has concluded that buyers tend to spend more if they can pay with a credit card. That's good business for you!

- **Pro**: Credit card payments can be authorized and verified quickly, allowing for fast availability of funds or immediate notification of a denied transaction.

- **Pro**: Faster availability of funds allows the seller to ship merchandise right away and close the deal faster.

- **Con**: Accepting credit cards in the traditional sense requires establishment of a merchant account at a bank or other sponsoring financial institution.

- **Con**: Traditional credit card processing carries a per-transaction fee as well as a sale percentage fee. Those fees cut into the seller's profit.

- **Con**: Sellers requesting a merchant account usually need to submit a lengthy application, withstand a rigorous personal credit check, and sometimes have their business established with their local city hall.

Accepting credit cards in the traditional way works well if yours will be an auction business with the look, feel, and maybe even the actual presence of a retail business. If you will spend your time in both the physical and virtual business markets, traditional accounts are still a good answer. However, be prepared for the traditional hoops you'll need to jump through to get properly established.

AuctionWatch.com has more!

If you want even deeper detail about merchant accounts, the fees, requirements, and providers, read AuctionWatch.com's tip online. Find it at http://www.auctionwatch.com/awdaily/tipsandtactics/sel-merchant.html

Buyer's Point of View

Buyers considering using a credit card by traditional means will have the following issues on their minds:

- **Pro**: It's easy—just like going to the store and saying "charge it."

- **Pro**: Most credit card issuers offer buyer protection plans and will assist a buyer in case of a transaction dispute.

- **Con**: Many buyers still worry about giving out their credit card information online.

- **Con**: Buyers realize (though not always) how quickly charges to their credit cards can add up to a hefty balance.

- **Con**: Depending on the monthly finance rate, the buyers can pay a lot of money in the long run if they carry a balance of the purchases on their card.

Online Payment Services

If your business will be strictly virtual or could fluctuate in volume from month to month, consider online payment systems—they make buying and selling using credit cards a whole lot easier. Online payment services are a booming trend for auction-goers. Below are the top players, who seem poised to make e-payment the natural choice.

Amazon.com Payments

Amazon.com acquired Accept.com in 1998 and renamed it Amazon.com Payments. This was a move to further bolster Amazon Auctions, offering credit card payment management for buyers at the auctions as well as at Amazon's zShops. There's no fee to buyers, but sellers pay a per-transaction fee as well as a percentage of the item's final value. This service is only for use at Amazon.com.

Billpoint

This online payment service has partnered directly with eBay to further promote its presence. Buyers pay no fee for credit card payments using Billpoint. Sellers, however, are charged when their customers choose this service (though still less than a traditional merchant account). Among its services, Billpoint offers a one-click payment system as well as an escrow-with-inspection service.

CCNow

Here's a provider that is positioned to assist the high-volume auctioneers and online merchants. In a much different approach from that used by other providers, CCNow actually buys merchandise from the seller and then resells it to the identified customer. For active sellers and online businesses, CCNow offers a wide variety of additional services and protections, but it does have a higher per-transaction fee.

Escrow.com

An affiliate of Fidelity National Financial and powered by Micro General's online escrow engine, this relative newcomer to the online payment game is another fee-based option for secure online escrow and payment. With 15 years of escrow experience for the real estate industry, escrow.com supports multiple payment forms, including credit card and wire transfer. Like other online escrow services, it verifies and secures the buyer's payment to the seller, and only releases payment to the seller after the buyer is completely satisfied with inspection of the merchandise.

i-Escrow

In 1999, this site became one of the pioneers of providing a safe way for auction-goers to buy and sell using credit cards. i-Escrow charges a fee (the buyer and seller have to decide who pays) but opens a traditional escrow account that gives sellers peace of mind that money's in the bank while offering buyers peace of mind that they can inspect an item before releasing funds. A drawback: sellers often complain that payment can take up to two weeks to arrive (via check).

ProPay.com

This relatively new service offers buyers and sellers another free alternative for processing true credit card transactions, online or in person. Also, unlike other payment systems that require both the buyer and seller to have an account, a ProPay.com Commerce Account allows sellers to accept a buyer's credit card without being a member of ProPay.com.

Tradesafe.com

This veteran online escrow service is also a secure credit card processor, online or in person. Providing quick, convenient credit card purchasing and protection against fraud and misrepresentation via a money-back guarantee for buyers, Tradesafe.com also remits payments to sellers immediately for transactions up to $1200, without the waiting period normally associated with traditional escrow services.

X.com/PayPal

Now a part of X.com, PayPal offers free online payment service. The service also offers $5 signup and referral rewards. Sellers can have money direct-deposited into their PayPal account, a specified bank account, or made payable to them in a check mailed to the seller.

Pros and Cons of Online Payment?

The benefit and drawbacks of online payment need to be determined by you as you review the different payment services and decide which one best suits your needs. The apprehension some folks have about online payment services is really only due to the relative "newness" of these services.

Online payment is a new trend but it certainly doesn't appear to be any sort of fleeting fad. There's much competition among online payment providers, and that's good news for buyers and sellers. When you decide to add online payment to your payment policy, be sure you can answer yes to these three key questions:

- Is payment fast? Can the buyer pay quickly? Can the seller receive funds quickly?

- Is payment easy? Whether buyer or seller, people don't like to monkey with difficult Web sites and convoluted terms and fees.

- Is payment safe? Though the real answers will come with time, be sure the payment service provides proper data protection for both buyer and seller.

Cash Payment

Yes, cash is still around. For online purchases, however, it's not a good option. For small purchases, it could be okay (rather than writing a check or buying a money order, if the seller doesn't accept credit cards or online payment). However, it's not traceable, it's not recoverable, and it's generally not very safe for buyers *or* sellers. In your payment policy, don't even mention cash. If you receive payment in the form of cash, ship that item immediately! With a tracking number!

Everything Else

So how about bank transfers, wire transfers, and C.O.D. (Collect On Delivery)? They're still out there, but these days they are somewhat out of date. With the payment methods already discussed, you'll be more than able to meet the needs of practically all of your customers.

International Payments

It's not necessarily a different type of payment, but don't forget your friends from around the world. International sales are a bit more difficult simply because they require special considerations as currencies are exchanged. You'll never need to worry about conversion rates, though, if you simply request an International Money Order. Whether your buyer is in Japan, Germany, or Timbuktu, International Money Orders can be cashed at any U.S. Post Office or can be deposited at most U.S. financial institutions.

 AuctionWatch.com has more! _____

For more on this topic, see AW's Selling Internationally tip , at http://www.auctionwatch.com/awdaily/tipsandtactics/sel-bounce.html

Shipping and Handling

Shipping and handling are those two annoying twins that enter into every auction transaction. Why annoying? Simply enough, they add cost for a buyer and effort for a seller. Though you can't avoid them, you can control them. As a seller defining an S&H policy, begin by determining what each term means to *you* and how you will communicate that to your customers.

- **Shipping**. This is the cost a carrier charges to deliver a package. There will be additional costs for extra services—insurance, tracking, delivery confirmation, and so on. Shipping costs vary from carrier to carrier.

- **Handling**. This one can be a bit ambiguous—handling involves your work to prepare an item for shipment. It could simply be a consideration of time spent but could also include recognition of the cost of packing materials (boxes, packing foam, tape, and so on). Why is it ambiguous? Buyers are usually unclear on why they must pay a handling fee, and what exactly that fee covers.

What Buyers Need to Know about S&H

Once defined, the shipping and handling charges need to be communicated to potential buyers *before* they bid on your auction. Here's what buyers will be looking for:

- Is handling being charged? Most buyers don't like such add-ons (considering your labor and supplies to be your cost of doing business); many sellers feel they should be duly compensated here. It's a decision that's up to each seller.

- Is the shipping cost calculated per item or as a flat rate? Some sellers specify flat rates that will cover the cost of shipping though usually the actual carrier charge is lower. The flat rate is usually a seller convenience though it does benefit a buyer by announcing the shipping cost and putting a ceiling on it. The alternative is for the shipping charge to be calculated at the time payment is due.

- Which carrier service will be used? Different carriers offer different levels of service, manage packages differently, have different delivery lead times, and offer different additional services. Buyers want to know whom the carrier will be so that they'll know how their item will be delivered, and what reasonable costs for delivery are.

- Are special delivery services optional? Buyers want to know if they have a choice regarding insurance, tracking, and confirmations. Since the cost will be passed on to them, it's reasonable they be given the option to accept or decline. Of course, buyers need to understand that they'll be responsible for the choices they make here (if they decline to pay for insurance and the package arrives damaged, for example, their earlier choice might leave them no recourse).

How Does Your S&H Policy Stack up?

That being said, you'll need to define your shipping and handling policy clearly and fairly. When you've done that, check to see how well your policy holds up under this scrutiny:

- Is the policy clear about who pays shipping costs?

- Is the policy clear about which carrier will be used and whether the buyer has a choice?

- Is the policy flexible enough to respond to the reasonable needs or requests of a buyer?

- Is the policy clear about any and all services that are being charged to the buyer?

- Is the policy clear about who will be responsible for loss or damage?

AuctionWatch.com has more!

For more on this topic, see AW's Stating Shipping Terms tip, at http://www.auctionwatch.com/awdaily/tipsandtactics/sel-ship.html

Establishing Your S&H Boundaries

A shipping and handling policy can be difficult to manage. Though you want to be in the service of your customers, you must take control of this part of doing auction business in order to ensure that you can develop a rhythm in your efforts while controlling your time and expense. Taking control means establishing some boundaries or parameters to your shipping policy. Try to incorporate these aspects:

- Settle on one primary and one secondary carrier for your shipping needs.

- Choose carriers who offer a wide range of services at the most reasonable costs.

- Choose carriers who offer inexpensive or free packing supplies—and *don't* charge a "supplies" fee.

- Choose carriers who can pack an item for you if it is particularly challenging. This might be an additional expense that you and the buyer agree will be added to the item's purchase price.

- Choose carriers who deliver quickly. Fast delivery means a happy buyer and a completed transaction.

Finally, your shipping and handling policy should state *when* you will ship items. Buyers who are sending money to you want to know when they can expect to receive their items. Be sure to indicate whether items are shipped upon payment receipt (depending on the payment method) or if items are shipped certain days of the week.

Refunds and Guarantees

To some sellers, this is a no-brainer; to others, it's a real puzzle. The whole matter of refunds and guarantees involves risk. For sellers, it's a risk of taking a loss on a returned or damaged item or it's a loss of time, effort, and income if a buyer decides to back out of a purchase. For buyers, the risk involves the *lack* of return privileges: if they purchase the item and aren't satisfied with it for whatever reason, they're stuck without recourse.

There are pros and cons for both parties when it comes to refunds and guarantees:

- **Pro**: Buyers can bid and buy with confidence, knowing that the seller will stand behind the sale.

- **Pro**: Sellers often attract more buyers because of their stated promise to "make the sale right."

- **Pro**: Buyers see that the seller has nothing to hide and therefore might be willing to spend more for an item given the seller's obvious confidence in the merchandise being offered.

- **Pro**: Sellers develop an online reputation for being trustworthy and customer-focused.

- **Con**: A return for refund can cost a seller in the end, especially if an item is damaged and therefore cannot be resold for the same price.

- **Con**: Returns are often a recurring scam where dishonest buyers will swap similar items in their possession, sending back an inferior example and trying to pass it off for the one the seller originally sent. (See Chapter 6 for more about this particular scam.)

- **Con**: Some buyers will bid and purchase on a whim, but will return the item when they realize their mistake.

- **Con**: Some buyers will attempt a return weeks or months after receiving the item.

Announcing Your Refund and Guarantee Policy Up Front

Although there are obvious benefits to having a return policy, it can be something of a minefield for sellers. Regardless, your responsibility is to clearly state your policy.

If You Will Accept Returns

If you decide to offer a return policy, protect yourself in the following ways:

- State the time window for returns (for example, within 10 days).

- Indicate that all returns must be preceded by an e-mail request.

- State that returns will only be offered for same items in same condition as sent.

- State that all returns are subject to inspection.

- State whether postage costs will be refunded (usually not).

- State your turnaround time for providing refunded money.

AuctionWatch.com has more!

For more on this topic, see AW's Offering Refunds and Guarantees tip, at http://www.auctionwatch.com/awdaily/tipsandtactics/sel-refunds.html

If You Will Not Accept Returns

If you decide you'd rather not accept returns, do the following up front in order to avoid trouble down the road:

- State it clearly: item sold "as is" with no returns or refunds.

- Be sure you've been explicit about the item's content, condition, or any other information that provides clear and accurate depiction of the item. *Don't* be accused of misrepresenting a non-returnable item.

Your Policy at a Glance

It's time to wrap it all up into a sales policy that works for you and works for your customers. To give you a bit of a head start, here are a couple of sample policies you might want to adapt to your own use:

Buyers will please prepay plus postage. Payment required within 10 days after auction close. Payment made via money order, cashier's check, or online payment will gain immediate shipment upon payment receipt. Personal checks accepted but checks must clear before item is shipped—allow 10 days for checks to clear. Items will be shipped via USPS Priority Mail unless other arrangements are made. Exact postage cost will be calculated at end of auction, including any special delivery costs or services requested by winning bidder. Please indicate if insurance is desired. If insurance declined, winning bidder will be responsible for damage or loss. All items guaranteed to be as described and refunds are cheerfully granted within 10 days of delivery (pending prior notification of return and item subject to inspection). If there are any questions about these terms, please contact me for clarification prior to bidding. Thanks for your interest in my auction!

Or....

Buyer to prepay plus $5.00 shipping and insurance. Payment must be received within 10 days of auction close via money order, cashier's check, personal check, or online payment. Allow 10 days for personal check to clear. All items guaranteed to be as described and are sold "as is" with no warranty or return implied. If you have any questions, please feel free to ask prior to bidding. Thanks!

Of course, policies can be stated more succinctly or more elaborately. You'll need to decide what your terms will be and how you'll communicate them to your customers.

The Best Way to Post Your Policy

Following are some different ways to post your sales policy.

- In the body of your listing narrative. This is the most obvious place to list your sales policy. If you use a no-frills description (with simple text), add your policy after the description of the item.

- If you use HTML in your item description, consider posting your policy under a header "Payment and Shipping Policy" (or something similar). Also consider reducing the font size of your terms and conditions slightly to offset them from the item description—but don't make them so small that they're difficult to read.

- Linked to your listing. If you want to provide highly detailed terms, consider using an embedded HTML link that is clearly visible and labeled something like "Payment and Shipping Terms." The link will guide potential bidders to a separate Web page. Bidders will be able to easily find your terms without having the terms clutter up or overpower your auction description.

- Selected from the site's listing menu. Use the special "term selections" offered at many auction sites. Most sites have check boxes, radio buttons, and other selectors where you can "click and choose" your policies from an assortment of popular selections. If you need to augment your terms, make additional notations either in the body of the listing or linked to it.

AuctionWatch.com has more!

For more on this topic, see AW's Stating Terms of Service tip , at http://www.auctionwatch.com/awdaily/tipsandtactics/sel-tos.html

Sticking to Your Guns (While Staying Flexible)

No matter how clear your policy some folks will ask for special exceptions, considerations, and favors. How you respond is certainly up to you, but you'll do well to consider a few things up front:

- Is the special request being made being out of customer necessity or for the customer's convenience?

- Will fulfilling the request cost more (in effort or expense) than the item is worth?

- If asked, would you make this special allowance for more customers more often?

Most sustained business is often attributed to return customers. Therefore, that's what you'll need to consider if you decide to (or decide not to) flex your policy.

When You Just Can't Bend

If your policy is quite clear and you're not inclined to deviate from it, you'll need to respond to that effect when special requests come in:

- Explain to customers that your volume of business doesn't allow for very much special handling.

- Ask the customer why a certain policy condition of yours will not meet their needs. The answer could reveal that the customer isn't considering *your* needs; on the other hand, you might learn that one of your policy conditions does not meet a majority of your customers' needs—you'll want to adjust your policy.

- If you cannot accommodate the request, respond promptly and explain your position quickly and clearly.

- If a customer expresses dissatisfaction, advise not bidding on your auction; agree to cancel a bid of theirs with no retribution on either part if that helps.

- If the customer is a winning bidder, do your best to accommodate the situation just to complete the transaction.

- Review the content and context of your policy to ensure that it is clear and complete; feel justified in sticking to it.

Remember, serving your customers means understanding their needs and how well you're presently meeting them. Be open to altering your policies for sound reasons. However, don't allow yourself to be "nickeled-and-dimed" to death if a customer seems intent on redefining how you conduct business. In the end, it's still your call, but say it with a smile.

Key Watch Points

- Be sure you fully understand the terms and conditions of any auction you participate in, as a buyer or as a site user.

- As you develop your sales policy, try to remember your goal is not only to clarify your style of business but also to communicate an eagerness to work in a very straightforward manner with your customers.

- Your sales policy needs to clearly address the following key conditions:

  - *Payment* types accepted and a window when payment is expected.

  - *Shipping and handling* charges, if any (plus any special shipping services offered).

  - *Refund and guarantee* terms, if any. Be sure you're clear as to whether you'll accept returns or insist that sales will be "as is."

- Post your policy clearly in the body of an auction listing, on a linkable Web site, or through use of a site's unique listing tools (or a combination of these methods). Whichever you choose, be sure the customer can quickly and easily find your whole policy.

- Review your policy and be open to customer response and requests. A customer who requests a deviation might have a valid need you can fulfill; such a request can also be an indicator that your policy is in need of revision.

- Feel comfortable in sticking to your policy terms. Work to the best of your ability to be accommodating, but don't be a doormat.

- Remember that sales policies should strive to create a win-win situation; they're designed to make both buyer and seller happy and confident in any transaction.

CHAPTER 5

Getting Organized

Level:	Beginner to Intermediate
Reader:	Seller

Whether you intend to dabble at the auctions or go full bore, organization will be the key to your success and the preservation of your sanity. Here is where you'll learn the importance of getting your ducks in a row and getting your business to move in formation. Most important, it's where you'll establish yourself and your routine. Though you needn't go overboard in organization, you will find that a little extra efficiency can significantly add to your eventual success and profit.

The Auction Office

Office, sweet office. Many have dreamed of a workplace away from the workplace. With online auctions, folks are finding income opportunities literally at their fingertips. However, when it's time to get serious about keeping the online income flowing, then it's time to set up serious shop. A first step is to establish an "auction office." But where? Here are a few ideas that could be right under your nose (or down the hall and to the right).

- **The extra room**. If your home or apartment has an extra room used for storage, clean it out and use it as a virtual store front instead. The extra room converted to a home office is typically the most desirable situation for managing auction activity; it's a self-contained work area that can go undisturbed and can be closed off when it's not in use.

- **Attic or basement**. These are the other natural "extra spaces" that are prime for home office conversion. Sometimes special considerations need to be taken when using an attic or basement (consider adequate head-room, lighting, protection from excessive heat or moisture), and a pre-inhabitation bug bomb could be in order.

- **A cozy corner**. If you can't devote an entire room, is there a special area of a room where you can set up shop? Workspaces can be located in the corner of a living room, dining room, or family room (or any room, for that matter). Typically all it takes is about eight square feet of dedicated space and you're in business.

- **A spare closet**. Believe it or not, standard wardrobe closets make excellent work areas. A typical six-foot closet provides ample floor space for locating a desk, chair, and the other office tools you'll soon learn about. The bonus of a closet, as with a spare room, is that they usually have doors that you can close to hide the workspace from view when not in use.

Why Bother with a Static Workplace?

In this mobile-technology culture, you might wonder why you should set up an office if you can be on the go. Sure, a laptop is an option, but it's typically not a good choice for long-term auction business. Mobile computing and communication look great in advertisements and are impressive at the espresso bar, but there are some drawbacks to not having an established workplace.

Connectivity

Connecting to the Internet can be twitchy when it comes to mobile computing. Repeated tries to connect to the Net with a cell-modem are definite time-wasters. Though connection isn't 100 percent guaranteed at all times in a permanent work area, odds say you'll do better than if you attempt to run your business while you're on the go.

Continuity

When you look at someone's messy desk, you may wonder how they ever get anything done. However, the occupant is typically quick to proclaim that they know *exactly* where everything is and *exactly* where they left off. A mobile environment doesn't support starting and stopping very well. The work needs to be packed up and put away, usually disrupting a natural flow in process. Plus, it's easier to lose important information, whether physical or virtual, in a transient environment.

Convenience

Though mobile computing is much ballyhooed as convenience in the palm of your hand, it's not very convenient to *have* to work from the palm of your hand. Serious auction-goers need to be able to spread out, to know that their office space is always ready and waiting for them, and, most importantly, they need to know that it's *their* space that can be cordoned off from other hands.

Claiming Expense

In Chapter 15, "Register, Report, and Deduct: The Pros and Cons of Being a Business," you'll learn how your permanent office space can also serve as a regular business deduction come tax time. If you work on the go, you lose the opportunity to shave a bit off your income liability.

The Bare Necessities

So, when you locate your prime office real estate, be sure it will have the basic amenities you'll need to get into business and stay productive.

- **Online access**. You need a phone line or cable line available or you won't be able to get onto the Net. Be sure live access is nearby, preferably on the same wall as where you'll locate your work surface. Of course, wireless access is up and coming, but at this time it's a bit too costly when compared to hard-wire connectivity.

- **Proper lighting**. Mom was right about eyestrain; it's no fun. Though a PC monitor has a glow all its own, you'll need decent overhead lighting as well as desk lighting to keep your eyesight from suffering and to keep all your work materials within easy view.

- **Elbow room**. Though it's not necessary to have a 20'×20' office to be effective, you do need a certain amount of space in which to work. Be sure you have a work surface that offers at least a 4'×3' work area (the more the better). Think about the PC monitor, the printer, the telephone, and many of the other office tools you'll need and want within easy reach.

- **Air circulation**. In most situations, this isn't much of a problem. However, if you're eyeballing the attic, the basement, or the garage, be sure you can maintain a comfortable room temperature and airflow. Avoid areas subject to extremes in temperature, static air, moisture, or dust.

AuctionWatch.com has more!

For more on this topic see AW's Setting Up Your Auction Office tip, at http://www.auctionwatch.com/awdaily/tipsandtactics/sel-office.html

Tools of the Trade

You've got your space, now it's time to fill it with the tools you'll need (and want) to shift your business into high gear. To start, consider the following:

- **Computer**. Technology has become incredibly inexpensive these days. Purchase a computer with at least a Pentium II chip in it (or an equivalent), and be sure you have at least 32MB of RAM, a hard drive that can store at least 3GB of data, and a modem that supports 56 Kbps. Actually, these are current low-end specifications. The faster and more robust your PC is, the faster and more efficient you'll be in your work. Expect to spend at least $1,000 for a decent PC—but expect that money to buy more and better technology with each passing month.

- **Printer**. Though it's an electronic age, there's still a need for printed matter. These days, printers are being bundled with PC packages and can be had, PC and all, for around that $1,000 price point. If you buy a stand-alone PC, expect to pay at least $150 for a printer, depending on your needs and wants. For your auction business, a simple color inkjet printer should meet your needs for years.

- **Telephone**. Though the phone in the kitchen is just around the corner or down the stairs, having a phone at your work area is a real convenience and time saver. Keep a phone pad and pencil nearby, too.

- **Internet access**. No matter where you live, there's an ISP (Internet Service Provider) nearby, ready to help you get online. Do some shopping to see who has the best rates ($19.95/month or less) and what additional services they offer (e-mail accounts, free Web space, and so on). And be sure to scrutinize the provider's support structure and customer assistance hours.

- **E-mail account**. This will be your key communication tool and it's typically free. You can either get free e-mail service with an ISP, or you can sign up for free e-mail accounts with online services such as AuctionWatch.com, Yahoo!, MSN Hotmail, Bigfoot, and others.

The Enhancing Extras

Now, add the gadgets that offer added convenience, comfort, and efficiency:

- **A second phone line**. There was a time when folks hooked up second lines to support a teen's talking habits. Today, second lines are almost indispensable for maintaining efficient access to the Internet while allowing another line to be free for making phone calls.

- **Hands-free phone system**. Though you might not consider this much more than a showy little upgrade, using a phone earpiece or headset really makes a difference. By keeping both hands free to type or maneuver a mouse, you can remain productive while you're on hold or in the middle of a conversation. Speakerphones and PC phones achieve the same thing, but the sound quality is often lower for both you and the person on the other end.

- **Postal scale**. Though postage will be covered a bit later, consider purchasing a postal scale for your auction office. These days, there are many from which to choose. Some simply weigh items and indicate postage cost while others have digital readouts and can print metered postage via a phone hookup.

- **Digital camera**. If you're selling, you want bidders looking. Bidders want to look at pictures and many will look away if they can't visually inspect the things you're offering. Digital cameras start at around $250. Look for ease of use, ease of image retrieval and upload, and image quality.

- **Scanner**. Though digital cameras can photograph anything, sellers who deal in flat items prefer scanners because they produce better image quality. Scanners, like other technology, are dropping in price all the time. You can find a decent one for as low as $100.

- **Image editing software**. With all this talk of images, a good software package to prepare your photos is beneficial. Many digital cameras and scanners come with free image editors that will get you started. If you want all the bells and whistles, you'll need to buy a package to better serve your needs. Commercially available software packages range in price so shop around (check out the upgrade offers that came with your camera or scanner), and don't forget to shop online, too.

- **Tripod**. Here again, with images being so important to your potential auction success, a simple camera tripod can pay for itself. It will help increase your image quality by decreasing the effect of camera movement.

- **Advanced e-mail programs**. Free e-mail is great, but some folks want more power in their communication. E-mail applications such as Eudora or Outlook Express give you even greater ability to file your messages, sort them, manage embedded files and applications and so much more than your basic, low-frills, Net browser tools.

Online Management Services

The real benefit offered to auction-goers today is the emergence of AuctionWatch.com, which is devoted to providing not only up-to-date information about the Internet and online auctions, but also a robust selection of professional auction management tools within its Auction Manager suite. Auction Manager's selection of online tools and complementary offline *bulk lister,* Auction Manager Pro, expedite every aspect of the auction listing and fullfillment process and enable auction enthusiasts and established businesses to sell their merchandise with greater ease and efficiency.

AW Auction Manager Pro

Launch hundreds of auctions simultaneously with this downloadable auction management tool. It's a *bulk lister;* that is, it allows you to prepare multiple listings offline to upload and launch later. Auction Manager Pro also features support for free image hosting, unique counter styles, and professional templates that simplify the auction creation process.

Auction Manager Pro also acts as your offline auction database, providing sellers with an application in which to enter and maintain inventory data and images for future listings; you can also monitor available, sold, and unsold quantities of merchandise and track prices realized. And for those still using a spreadsheet program to record inventory and sales information, AM Pro's new "Inventory Importer" allows sellers to import data from their spreadsheets into an AM Pro "Inventory List."

Learn more about Auction Manager Pro at http://www.auctionwatch.com/ help/ampro/ampro-howto _v20.html

Control Panel

Review and manage all of your auction activity from a single location. If you're selling, this tool provides an organized view of your active auctions, including their current "hits" and "bids." You also can review closed auctions and auctions you've scheduled for a later start. If you're buying, you can import the auctions you've bid on and monitor their progress up to and after close.

Create Auction

If you're interested in creating your auctions at a more relaxed pace, this tool makes it easy to design and launch your auction at one of several major auction sites. Choose from different template styles, add images, and include counters to make your auction stand out and monitor the number of times it has been viewed by prospective bidders.

Inventory Management

A great tool for high-volume sellers and businesses that sell similar items on a regular basis. Enter your item once, and it's ready to launch on multiple auction sites over and over again, whenever you please. The AW Inventory Management system allows you to create and organize thousands of items. We'll discuss Inventory Management's features in more detail in Chapter 11, "Establishing and Managing Your Inventory."

Track Auction

Whether you're buying for resale or buying for yourself, use this tool to watch an auction, whether you've bid yet or not. Track active auction by lot number or by seller. It saves time and effort, freeing you from having to remember which site you were browsing when you saw that special item or terrific investment opportunity.

Customer Management

Generate future sales leads by automatically collecting and storing contact information on everyone who places a bid on your auctions. Keep these customers apprised of new auctions that will interest them and provide losing bidders with another chance to bid on that item they didn't win.

Learn more at http://www.auctionwatch.com/help/acp/crmtool-howto.html

Post Sale Management

Here's a truly innovative tool set that aids sellers by automating the end-of-auction notification and fulfillment process. It collects responses to your winning bidder notifications and notifies you when winners have responded, enables you to print out professional packing slips and invoices, automates feedback posting, and track previous post-sale activity from one location.

Learn more at http://www.auctionwatch.com/help/acp/psmtool-howto.html

Auction Toolkit

If you're looking for assistance and services to help manage payment receipt, item shipping, and insurance options, this toolkit puts them all within easy reach to make your end-of-auction effort virtually effortless.

Universal Search

Good sellers know to keep an edge on the auction market by keeping an eye on what's being auctioned and what prices are being paid. This search tool puts more power behind your searches by pulling down results from several major auction sites with a single click of the mouse and then tracking specific ones from your Auction Manager Control Panel. Sellers also can purchase "Featured Results" placements within Universal Search to give their listings added exposure. Sellers and buyers also will profit from the new Image Gallery, offering images with select search results.

Staging Your Auction Items

Remember the earlier discussion about your auction office and your dedicated auction workspace? Besides serving as a constant home to your auction tools (the PC, printer, and all the rest), your auction space also can serve as your auction "staging area." When you list your goods and treasures for sale in the virtual marketplace, your glowing descriptions aren't enough—you have to deal with the goods themselves before, during, and after the auction. So why might you need a specific auction staging area?

- A staging area provides space to examine, categorize, and catalog your auctionable merchandise.

- A staging area can serve as a mini photography studio where you take digital pictures of your items.

AuctionWatch.com has more! _____

For more on this topic see AW's Taking Better Photos tip, at http://www. auctionwatch.com/awdaily/tipsandtactics/sel-photos.html

- A staging area can also serve as a safe storage area to keep items clean and free from damage or loss. This is especially important if they're currently being bid on or are ready for shipment.

- A staging area can provide further organization to your auction business, eliminating clutter and enabling you to deal with your merchandise faster and more efficiently.

Staging Area Basics

A staging area doesn't necessarily need to be in the same place as your auction office, though it's preferable in terms of keeping all the auction activity in one central location. Many auctioneers use different rooms or storage areas for their staging and storing needs. Whichever approach you choose, be sure your staging area meets these requirements:

- It should be clean, dry, and free from temperature extremes.

- It should be clearly identifiable as a devoted staging and storage area to prevent others from moving or removing merchandise you intend to sell or are currently auctioning.

- It should be spacious enough to accommodate the goods you intend to auction without being crammed or overstuffed, the leading cause of post-auction damage.

- It should be easily accessible to you, allowing you to get to your merchandise without climbing over stacks of boxes, crouching into crawlspaces, and creeping up shaky ladders.

Remember, the key to becoming organized and staying that way is to develop work areas that are easy to work in and to work with.

The Supply Room

Free yourself from rummaging for the last roll of tape or endlessly searching for the right box for an item. You need a supply room that will be well stocked with all the goods you need to make the easy transition from listing an item to packing an item.

Establishing a Supply Room

Though you might be anticipating this by now, be sure your supply room has the following qualities:

- It's a dedicated area. A single auction office located in a spare room can serve multiple auction uses (office, staging area, supply room). In fact, if you can find a large enough living space, the best auction environment is one where *all* of your auction activity can be contained within a single space. If not, find another corner where you can set up a supply shop.

- It's a clean and well-lit area. Cleanliness and good lighting will work in your favor as you pack up those items that customers have already paid for and are anxiously awaiting.

- It's large enough to allow organization. A mansion isn't necessary, but you'll do better if all your supplies aren't stacked in a cramped corner or dumped into a carton that requires upending for you to get to what you need.

- There's adequate workspace in which to pack items. It's where you'll keep your supplies and where you should expect to use them, too. Make sure you have enough room to work.

Stocking a Supply Room

Now you need supplies. What supplies? Here's the laundry list of things every well-stocked supply room should have:

Boxes

You can get them in all shapes and sizes these days; many are designed to hold specific kinds of items (videotapes, for example) and keep them safe. Most of these are free from carriers such as USPS or UPS. Store them flat so they take up less space.

Mailing Tubes

If you'll be shipping rolled items, you'll want tubes or special tubelike mailing boxes. They're also free from many shippers. If they're the box type, you can store them flat. If they're actual tubes, store them in a half-box to keep them contained but easy to use.

Box Fill

You know it as packing peanuts and environment-friendly Eco-Foam and it's some of the best lightweight material to fill a box and provide necessary interior cushioning. Wadded or shredded paper also works fine but it tends to be costly if a large amount is required. Box fill can take a bit more space to store; consider a large box or a clean garbage bag in which to store it. Some people hang it from the ceiling and dispense it from a reclosable "spout." Neat.

Bubble Pack

This is excellent for wrapping items and adding an extra layer or protection (both for cushioning and cleanliness) to items. Sheets of varying size can be stored in a box; bigger quantities can be rolled on a spindle.

Tape

Lots of it. Store your tape in a drawer or on peg hooks for easy view and easy access. You'll want different types of tape for different needs:

- Wide shipping tape (clear or otherwise, used for sealing and reinforcing boxes)

- Brown paper tape, pregummed and often with filament reinforcement— also used for sealing or reinforcing boxes

- Masking tape or cellophane tape for securing interior packing such as bubble wrap around an item

Backing Board and Stiffener

Smaller sheets and sections of cardboard (either corrugated or chipboard) are useful for providing interior stiffening to prevent bends and creases for flat items. This can be stored in a suitable–sized box or a drawer.

Envelopes

Have a good assortment of these, ranging from standard letter-sized envelopes up to (and beyond?) heavy-duty 9"×12" manila envelopes. Padded envelopes are also good but are comparatively costly and the protection they provide can be gained by using a combination of cheaper materials (such as stiffener or bubble pack in a manila envelope). Store envelopes in a box or drawer.

Mailing Labels

Again, these are now free from most carriers and most of them—even USPS Priority Mail—will arrange to have your return address preprinted on them for even easier use. Store labels in a drawer or on a shelf.

Supply Shop Tools

These are the other things you'll need (though not necessarily in bulk) in your supply shop:

- Bold waterproof marking pens
- A utility knife
- Scissors
- Blank white paper (for notes or correspondence)

Organizing a Supply Room

The key to organization is to have what you need, when you need it, and within easy reach. As you establish your supply room, envision the actual flow of work. Picture an assembly line process (moving from left to right) or a single-item packing station where all packing materials are within reach (boxes underneath, box fill up above, tape to the left, labels to the right). Though it might sound a bit silly, the organization of your supply room is what will allow you to develop a repeatable and time-efficient packing process.

AuctionWatch.com has more!

If you want know more about actual packing techniques, read these AuctionWatch.com tips.

Packing Merchandise:

http://www.auctionwatch.com/awdaily/tipsandtactics/sel-pack.html

More Pointers on Packing:

http://www.auctionwatch.com/awdaily/tipsandtactics/ sel-morepack.html

Point of Departure: Which Carrier Should You Choose?

You might be wondering how choosing a package carrier will affect your over-all auction organization. Keep in mind that dropping off packages for delivery is still another step in your business process and is sometimes a time-hungry one at that. Since different carriers offer different services, first consider which services will be most useful to you.

- Does the carrier have a local office or drop-off station? Time on the road is time away from your business. Though most carriers have many service offices, use proximity as one of your deciding criteria—the closer the better.

- Does the carrier provide pick-up services? What's better than having a drop-off point just around the corner? How about a drop-off point that's as close as your doorstep? Some carriers provide this service, sometimes at a fee but often for free.

- Does the carrier deliver packing supplies? Though it's more on the front-end of shipping a package, determine if the carrier will deliver the supplies you need right to your door.

- What are the carrier's regular office hours? Expect that you'll visit the carrier at one time or another. Does the carrier have convenient weekday hours (outside the normal 9 to 5 when you might be working at another job)? Does it have weekend hours?

- Is the carrier's office well-staffed? You definitely want to choose a carrier with a well-trained and helpful staff, but you also want to be sure there will be more than one person standing at the counter lest you find yourself wasting precious time standing in a long line.

- Is the carrier competitively priced compared to other carriers? Price can affect your efficiency when it causes you to go out of your way or expend extra effort to keep costs under control. Naturally, you'll want to pack effectively to control shipping costs, but if you find yourself bending over backward to beat the carrier's rates, you might consider choosing a more cost-friendly carrier.

AuctionWatch.com has more!

For more on this topic, read AW's Dealing With Damaged Goods and Picking Postage tips, at

http://www.auctionwatch.com/awdaily/tipsandtactics/buy-damage.html

and

http://www.auctionwatch.com/awdaily/tipsandtactics/sel-post.html

Time Management

And at the end of the day, you'll want to know that all your hard work to get organized is paying off by affording you more time to get more done (not to mention more time to relax). Time management is no longer just a corporate concern. As more and more people begin to find alternative sources of income and opportunities to work from their homes, good time management reinforces the age-old axiom, "Time is money."

Tangible Time-saving Strategies

Several tools and techniques exist that will save you both time and effort in your auction endeavors.

Use Bulk Listers

You'll save significant time if you upload auctions in volume rather than one at a time. If you're going to be listing a lot of items week after week, let a bulk lister help ease some of the burden.

Create and Use Templates

Set up a pattern document that you can use as a base for your listings, plugging in specific details for each auction item. It doesn't have to be perfect to start with; if you prefer, make use of the AuctionWatch templates and don't bother authoring your own. If you're using a bulk lister, expect that it will include a template framework of its own. In addition, consider e-mail templates that will save you time in your correspondence. No sense in writing the same sentences over and over again.

Develop a Database

Keep track of your inventory, sales, and customer records with a software application designed specifically for that purpose. Filing and retrieving information in a database is far more time-efficient than searching through e-mail or stacks of sticky notes.

Check Your Hardware

Is your PC out of date? If so, it could be robbing you of precious time as you wait for it to execute tasks that newer PCs simply whiz through. This can be a costly upgrade, but weigh how that cost might be offset by increased productivity and increased sales.

AuctionWatch.com has more! _____

For more on this topic see AW's Timesaving Strategies tip, at http://www. auctionwatch.com/awdaily/tipsandtactics/sel-timesave.html

The Intangibles

Now, consider some of the strategies that can save or cost you hours every day of every week of every year. These time-savers are more related to your business behavior, but they're often the ones that can bring the greatest returns in the long run.

Establish Working Hours

At the auctions, you're the boss, so set your own hours. Whether you choose to work hours on end or at segmented times of the day, put a schedule in place when work is to be done and do it. Many home business enterprises fail due to lack of discipline in setting regular working hours.

Stay in Your Office

With so many products and resources now available online, you can save time that was once wasted driving here and there. Today, you can order packing supplies online, you can buy postage online, and you can research your customer market online. What a time-saver!

Limit Interruptions

If your friends keep calling to chat, switch over to the answering machine. If "you've got mail" throws you off-track, close your e-mail window. If there's a television in your auction office, leave it off or get it out of the room. You'll soon realize why traditional employers prefer the standard office space when it comes to productivity.

Develop a Weekly Work Schedule

Monday is e-mail day. Tuesday is listing day. Wednesday is packing day. Whatever schedule works best for you, develop it into a routine so you can anticipate the next day's duties and avoid wasting time pondering, "Hmm. What should I do today?"

Focus on the Task at Hand

While you're working the auctions online, it's all too easy to become distracted and surf off to read, play, or shop. Stick to your task until it's done, and *then* play.

Take a Break

Okay. *Now* it's playtime. Yes, time off can be an incredible productivity boost and can save you from wasting time daydreaming or generally feeling sluggish and burnt out. Get away for lunch. Take a midday exercise break. Get up and stretch for ten minutes. Take regular breaks not only for your physical well-being (get out of that desk chair once in a while) but also for your mental well-being. It's been proven that regular, but not excessive, breaks serve as a mental reenergizer, allowing you to return to work with a refreshed perspective and renewed motivation.

Key Watch Points

- Good organization begins with a place to work. Establish your own auction office and set up shop to best suit your needs.

- Be sure you have the proper tools to enable your auction business to be efficient and effective.

- Be sure to take advantage of the many tools and helpers at AuctionWatch.com; they're there for you.

- Be sure you have dedicated auction staging, storage, and shipping areas. Dedicated areas allow you to establish a routine and an efficient flow.

- Establish regular use of time-saving tools and time-thrifty work habits. The time you save can literally translate to money in the bank.

CHAPTER 6

Fraud: The Sale That Went South

Level: *Advanced*

Reader: *Buyers and Sellers*

Sometimes, bad things happen to good people and at good places. Online auctions are not immune to the misdeeds and misconduct of the few. In fact, online auctions were named the number one source of Internet fraud in 1998 and 1999 by the National Consumers League. Still, that doesn't mean that *everyone* you deal with should be treated with suspicion. Take heart—99 percent of the time your transactions will come off just fine, whether you're the buyer or the seller. However, if trouble is going to rear its ugly head, you'll want to be aware and prepared. Here, then, is your quick course in online auction crime busting.

The Top Ten Frauds at Online Auctions

Begin by understanding the common scams that occur in the auction place, what signs can tip you off to a scam in progress, and, what you can do to thwart the evil doer.

Fraud #1: Bid Shilling

The Scam: A dishonest seller will make use of multiple user IDs or will enlist associates to place bogus bids so as to unfairly and falsely raise the number of bids received and the price of an item. This scam is perpetrated by sellers who are looking to artificially increase the bidding activity and increase their final sales price.

Warning Signs

Here are a few ways to spot a possible shill operation in action:

- Watch for recurring user IDs that are used to place bids on several of a particular seller's auctions.

- Watch for a recurring pattern in which the same bidder or bidders place last-minute bids on a particular seller's auctions.

- Watch for bidders and sellers who regularly bid on one another's auctions (especially if they never appear to win).

Protective Measures

If you think you've been the target of a shill bidding operation, report the incident to the hosting site immediately; provide any supporting evidence, such as other auctions, where you believe the seller employed shilling. Your best bet for prevention is to make note of an apparent shill seller or bidder and avoid that person's auctions in the future.

Fraud #2: Bid Shielding

The Scam: A ring of dishonest bidders (or a bidder using multiple user IDs) targets an item and inflates the high bid value to scare off other potential bidders. At the last moment, the high bidder or bidders retract their bids, thus allowing the lower-bidding ring partner to win the item at the once again low—and dishonest—price. The innocent seller has been cheated out of a higher price and other bidders have been falsely steered away from a potential win.

Warning Signs

Following are ways to determine if bid shielders are afoot:

- Watch for a bidder who seems to have a pattern of bidding and then retracting near the end of the auction.

- As with shilling, watch for patterns of apparent partnerships or use of multiple user IDs that tend to bid on the same items or one another's items.

Protective Measures

As with shilling, report a suspected shield to the hosting site immediately. Make note of bidders who appear to be involved in repeated shielding and cancel their bids.

Fraud #3: Fake Photos and Misleading Descriptions

The Scam: In this one, sellers falsely embellish or distort the presentation of the items they're auctioning. Borrowed images, ambiguous descriptions, and falsified facts are some of the tactics a seller will employ when lacking confidence, knowledge, or good judgment. The eventual buyer will typically receive an inferior item that doesn't match what was promised and isn't worth the bid price.

Warning Signs

To spot a snake–oil salesman doing his thing, try the following:

- Watch for item descriptions that seem too good to be true.

- Watch for disparities between a written description and an embedded image of the item.

- Watch for ambiguous or incomplete descriptions.

- Watch for seemingly "borrowed" images (something that appeared in another auction just prior or concurrently; something that looks as if it was lifted from a commercial advertisement).

- Watch for heavily touched-up photos.

Protective Measures

Be informed about the items you'll bid on. Carefully scrutinize all descriptive information including images. If you have any questions or hesitations, contact the seller to inquire. If the seller seems evasive, avoid the auction and the seller.

Fraud #4: Final Price Manipulation

The Scam: Here, the final price is not what it should be—perhaps you're asked to pay your *exact* bid for a Dutch auction purchase, instead of the lowest winning bid amount, or asked to pay your maximum bid if a previous high bidder retracted, even though your winning bid was registered at the site as just enough to beat the bidder below you. Alternatively, there may be superfluous "additional charges" tacked on—charges that were never previously disclosed and that don't make much sense.

Warning Signs

Really, price manipulation doesn't give you much advance warning since the costs requested by the seller come after the auction is over. However, be on the lookout for sales policies that ambiguously refer to odd or potentially excessive costs and end-of-auction prices.

Protective Measures

Your best protection is to quote the seller's policy back to him or her by return e-mail. If the seller seems confused as to the calculation of a final high bid (as in the case of Dutch auctions), refer the seller to the host site's rules. Do not pay if you believe price manipulation is occurring, and report the seller to the host site immediately. Avoid the seller in the future.

Fraud #5: Inflated Shipping and Handling Costs

The Scam: This one is akin to some aspects of Final Price Manipulation, though it can be somewhat more subtle. Perhaps a seller requests $5 for postage, but the item is something small and light that wouldn't cost more than $3.20 (if that) to ship. Sellers sometimes inflate postage and handling costs to garner a few extra dollars for themselves.

Warning Signs

Here's how to spot a dealer who's making an undo profit on shipping:

- Watch for sellers who charge a "handling" or "supplies" fee, especially when they use free packing supplies from the major carriers.

- Watch for sellers who charge flat rates for shipping and handling that seem beyond the acceptable norm (say, more than $5).

- Watch for sellers who charge high flat rates for small items, regardless of the item's size and weight.

- Watch for sellers who are evasive or unwilling to clarify their shipping and handling fees.

Protective Measures

Start by being sure you understand all fees you'll be asked to pay, then question any fees that seem excessive. Politely ask the seller to clarify fees and how those fees were derived. Request specific carriers (such as USPS) and quote to the seller what the cost should be for shipping and any other services. Avoid the seller in the future.

Fraud #6: Failure to Ship Merchandise

The Scam: Probably the most feared and enraging of all scams, in which the seller simply never sends the goods. The buyer pays up front in good faith, then waits and waits and waits for a package that never arrives. A dishonest seller might claim the item was shipped and has since been lost—but most often the seller fails to respond or communicate at all with the buyer though the buyer's money has already been taken.

Warning Signs

You typically aren't aware that you're about to be scammed until after you've sent your payment. But, here's the modus operandi of most non-shipping sellers:

- They are quick to make contact and request payment.

- They don't send confirmation that payment has been received.

- They don't reply, even after repeated attempts to contact them.

- They leave bogus contact information with the hosting site, so irate buyers can't get through to them by other means (phone, street address).

- They try to auction the same item again at the auction site, at a different auction site, or under a different user ID.

Protective Measures

The bottom line is that this is classic mail fraud and is high on the list at investigative agencies as well as at auction sites.

- Keep complete records of all correspondence, including any messages received from the seller when payment was requested.

- Be sure all correspondence you send to the seller is professional and nonthreatening.

- Make a final request to the seller and advise that you will turn the matter over to the proper authorities (start with the auction site and your Attorney General).

- When paying for items, try to use a credit card whenever possible: you will be able to dispute the charge and the card issuer will help you sort the matter out. But, let justice take its course and be on the lookout for this seller around the auction places.

Fraud #7: Selling Knock-Offs, Fakes, and Reproductions

The Scam: It looks like the real thing, it sounds like the real thing, and it might even smell like the real thing, but it's *not* the real thing. Knock-off, reproduced, and copycat goods make their way into the online auction marketplace every day. Sellers might claim it's real or might hedge a bit about authenticity, but these scammers know they're selling a cheap imitation and are hoping to catch a high-paying buyer who doesn't know how to spot a fake.

Warning Signs

You can spot merchandise that's too good to be true if your eyes are always kept freshly peeled.

- Watch out for truly rare and hard-to-find items suddenly appearing in pristine condition.

- Watch out for roundabout descriptions where sellers say they *think* it's the real thing or got it from another source who *said* it has to be authentic—no it doesn't, and it probably isn't.

- Watch out for sellers that can't seem to provide satisfactory information about the provenance of an item.

Protective Measures

It's a *caveat emptor* world at online auctions, so buyers need to know their stuff.

- Study up on the items you'll consider bidding on, especially if they have the potential to become quite expensive.

- Ask as many questions as you need in order to clearly identify the item—and beware the seller who cops an attitude of, "It's real, okay? So bid on it."

- If you receive an item that is not authentic, contact the seller immediately for a return and refund. If the seller "skips town," report the incident immediately.

Fraud #8: Improper Grading Techniques

The Scam: The seller states that the item is "definitely in excellent condition. A real '10' here." The item the buyer receives is less than perfect; it might be flawed or damaged or could even be incomplete. The seller has painted a rosy picture to bring in the bids, even though the goods aren't of the top quality needed to command a high-end price.

Warning Signs

Here's how to tell whether a seller is being "too generous" in his grading.

- The seller claims the item is in "100 percent mint condition." Even newly manufactured items usually bear some sort of imperfection.

- The description fails to offer full disclosure of the item's condition or completeness, especially when it's a well-known item and highly desirable.

- The seller has omitted critical details that are key to accurate grading of the particular item.

- Embedded images show signs of being altered, selectively photographed (only one side is displayed), or unnecessarily cropped where damage might be concealed.

Protective Measures

Grading can be very subjective depending on the grader's experience, expectations, and methods of comparison.

- Your best protection in cases of wrongful upgrading is to understand the item well, to be able to spot potentially problem areas quickly, and to ask specific questions about an item's condition.

- If an item is less than stellar when it was billed as exquisite, send it back.

- If you're concerned about purchasing an item based on its grading, ask if the seller offers return privileges. If not, then it's *caveat emptor* all over again.

Fraud #9: Phony Loss and Damage Claims

The Scam: A buyer contacts a seller to state that an item never arrived or was seriously damaged, even though the item may have arrived just fine. The buyer requests a refund and asks the seller to work out the details afterward.

Warning Signs

Here's how to tell if the buyer's hoping to ice the cake by getting his bid price back:

- A buyer contacts you weeks or months after the item was shipped to claim loss or damage.

- A buyer demands a refund immediately, before you've had sufficient time to assess the situation or involve the carrier for resolution.

- A buyer offers to throw a damaged item away for you since it won't be worth anything in such "bad" condition.

- A buyer is on record as having signed for or otherwise received an item that is now claimed to be lost in the mail.

Protective Measures

Again, another classic situation of mail fraud. Here's how to prevent falling prey:

- The best protection from false claims is to insure your outgoing goods or otherwise use tracking methods for all of your packages.

- Be sure the buyer is aware of his or her responsibility for loss and damage if insurance or tracking is declined (remember, the buyer should pay for these services).

- Keep all receipts and tracking numbers until you have confirmed with the buyer that the package arrived safely and the contents are in the same condition as when shipped.

Fraud #10: Switch and Return

The Scam: Some buyers will purchase an item, receive it, claim they're dissatisfied, and return it for a refund. However, the item they return is not the same item originally sent—it's of lesser quality or condition.

Warning Signs

Here's how to tell if an unscrupulous buyer is attempting to get a free upgrade:

- A buyer might seem overly interested in your return policy before he's bid or won.

- A buyer is vague about the reason for wanting to return an item.

- A buyer wishes to return an item after a significant lapse of time (weeks or months).

Protective Measures

Unfortunately, this scam is the key reason why many sellers do not offer return privileges. You can still accept returns, but indicate that all items must be inspected prior to issuing a refund. Your clear description and good images will serve as proof of intrinsic details of your item, which helps identify a swapped item that was dishonestly returned. If the return is an attempt at a switch, notify the buyer that the item is not the same one shipped and return it (accompanied by written clarification of points of dissimilarity) to the buyer. Bar the buyer from bidding in any of your future auctions.

Avoid the Rush to Judge

All that said—and with the exception of a few of the more blatant frauds noted—understand that some things that smell like scams are really not scams at all—they're the result of an inexperienced buyer or seller. Take a first step to inquire and clarify—you might end up helping another auction user get a grip on the ways and means of auctioning. You've got a scam on your hands if the other person becomes evasive, erratic, or irascible; such behavior indicates that their original intentions were probably not honorable.

Fee Refunds and Auction Insurance

Though it's useful to know how to spot, respond to, and avoid the top ten auction frauds, you're not altogether on your own. The auction sites are also very interested in keeping everyone happy. In cases where fraud has occurred, most major auction sites have instituted policies and programs to help you recover your loss and get you back on the auction path again. If fraud concerns you (and so it should), look into which sites are offering these sorts of "fraud offsets":

Fee Refunds

Determine what steps are required of you and what proof you have to provide in order to make a claim and collect your fee refund. Also inquire about the processing time to have your refund processed. A good protection program for defrauded sellers will include the following recoverable costs:

- Listing Fee

- Final Value Fee (the value price commission)

- Special Feature Fees (though some sites claim these are non-refundable)

Auction Insurance

Sites have acknowledged the risk involved with prepaying for an item and facing the possibility that it may never be sent. Therefore, some sites offer insurance under which a defrauded buyer will be reimbursed by the site (or a site's insurance affiliate) for the cost of the item purchased. Look for these distinguishing characteristics of an insurance program:

- Limitations on coverage (ceiling values, deductibles)

- Waiting periods before an insurance claim can be submitted

- Lead time from when the claim is made until the covered value is issued to the buyer

- Follow-up investigation to deal with the fraudulent seller

Plan of Action

Here's a summary of how to best protect yourself and how to properly respond to a fraud (or suspected fraud).

- Be informed: always be familiar with the rules at an auction site and especially with a particular auction format in which you're participating.

- Investigate: research sellers and buyers by investigating their feedback ratings and comments at the site; those numbers and notes will often quickly reveal if trouble might be just around the corner.

- Know your rights: be sure you understand how a site works with its users to combat fraud and how you're protected if you become entangled in a scam.

- Communicate: keep your communication flowing with the other person and be professional at all times, especially if you believe a scam is in the works.

- Be direct: if you suspect a scam (or at least a significant bending of site rules), indicate that to the other person and state how you will intend to complete (or terminate) the transaction.

- Follow through: if it's a scam, take action by reporting the incident to the site administrators, then consider taking the next step to report particularly flagrant scams to the proper authorities and organizations (more about what those are in the next section).

- Document and file: keep all correspondence concerning the incident as well as a record of how the events transpired. This is the sort of information that will be needed in the case of any investigation.

- Keep a positive outlook: don't become paranoid and suspicious; 99.9 percent of the time you'll enjoy simple and straightforward transactions with honest people.

Organizations on Your Side

Since auctions earned the undesirable reputation of being the Internet's number one haven for online fraud, several organizations have stepped forward to combat the problem. Here are some that could be helpful to you should one of your deals goes sour:

- Start with the hosting auction site. Most sites have implemented user protection services to help ward off fraud.

- Enlist a mediation service like SquareTrade (a service free to eBay users) that will pull together disputing parties to discuss and hopefully resolve the problem at hand.

- BBB Online (the Internet arm of the Better Business Bureau) has devoted itself to good business and consumer protection. Most major auction sites are members of BBB Online.

- Your Postmaster General and local Attorney General are always interested in fighting any sort of mail fraud. Contact them if you're in the middle of a rip-off that is of significant value.

- The National Consumer's League has formed the Internet Fraud Watch to hear consumer's problems specific to online dealings. NCL is a non-profit organization that's been assisting consumers with information and advice since 1899.

When It's Time to Take a Loss

Then there's a time when it's best to hang it up and walk away. That's difficult advice to give because it's difficult medicine to take. However, sometimes you could be better off just chalking it up to experience. Consider the following indicators of when you might be best served by simply eating the loss:

- The item you were buying was of low value.

- Feedback on the person indicated potential trouble and you chose to ignore it (never again, though).

- The cost—in time, effort, and money—to pursue the situation is far more than the item is worth, or more than it's worth to you.

- The organizations you've gone to for assistance indicate that your loss will be unrecoverable.

It's never pleasant to admit that someone else has gotten the better of you or has gotten away with an illicit deed. But convince yourself to move on and let the situation go if it seems no restitution is in sight, and be glad that you're now far more educated about the dirty games some people play.

Key Watch Points

- Always have clear understanding of the rules at any auction site and be clear about how those rules are enforced.

- Understand the methods and warning signs of the commonly perpetrated online auction frauds.

- Be alert and respond directly and professionally if you believe you might be getting pulled into a fraud scheme.

- Be clear about your intentions and communicate those to the other person if you believe it's time to report the apparent fraud (but *never* threaten).

- Enlist the assistance of the auction site and other organizations (when necessary) to thwart the fraud in progress.

- Be assured that fraud is still relatively rare when compared to the millions of transactions that take place at online auctions.

PART II
Polishing
Your Auction
Presence

Representing Yourself Like a Pro: Listing Effectively

Level:	Intermediate
Reader:	Seller

Now it is time to focus on the actual business at hand: auctioning. You've come to make money and that means selling merchandise. But selling at an online auction requires a thoughtful and deliberate approach if you're going to compete with the millions of other sellers clamoring for bidders' attention. So start from the beginning and understand the keys to effectively posting auction items in a way that will keep your great merchandise from being overlooked and underbid.

The Details of Differentiation

Initially, you need to consider *what items* you'll auction and how you'll establish yourself in bidders' minds. Many are content to play at the auctions, selling odds and ends in a sporadic manner. That's a fine and acceptable approach, but if you really want to establish a niche in the auction world, you'll need to develop a vision of what goods and services you'll provide and what sort of reputation you'd like to earn that, in turn, will earn you more customers.

Identify Your Commodity

Decide what it is that you'll sell and how often you'll be selling it. Consider what commodities will gain you the best ongoing success:

- Will your items be commonly available merchandise or rare and unique finds?

- Will your items be big-ticket (costly) items or low-dollar bargains?

- Can you ensure a perpetual replenishment of the items you'll want to sell or will they be catch-as-catch-can pieces?

- Will you specialize in a particular commodity or will you offer everything and anything (the General Store approach)?

- Is there much competition in the commodity you'll offer for sale, or will you truly be a treasure finder?

- Is there enough *demand* for your commodity to allow you to establish a certain level of sales and sales income?

- Can your commodity sustain customer interest or will you need to continually evolve and acquire new and different merchandise to maintain stable sales levels?

- Does your commodity lend itself to spin-off or companion goods that you can branch into over time?

- Will your merchandise be seasonal, experiencing predictable peaks and lulls in demand? (That's not a bad situation if you anticipate taking breaks from selling during the year.)

AuctionWatch.com has more!

For more on this topic, read AW's Selling for the Holidays and Selling Strategies for Spring Cleaning tips, at

http://www.auctionwatch.com/awdaily/tipsandtactics/sel-holiday.html

and

http://www.auctionwatch.com/awdaily/tipsandtactics/sel-clean.html

Identify Your Customers

You've chosen your commodity, now decide who will buy such items.

- Research the market to once again verify and validate the demand for this merchandise.

- Recognize the demographics of your potential customer base. (Mostly young people? Mostly older shoppers? Mostly investors?)

- Identify any special needs these customers might have, such as authentication, guarantees, unique information, or additional descriptive information.

- Determine whether your customer base can become a pool of repeat customers or if they'll be one-time buyers. (Either can be profitable, but it makes a difference to your approach.)

- Is your customer base constantly replenishing? Are new customers seeking your merchandise or do you serve a relatively static audience of buyers?

Identify Yourself

When you're new to the selling scene, you'll practically need to introduce yourself to the marketplace and your target customers.

- Make a splash with a generous number of initial listings to attract and pique the interest of customers.

- Develop a Web page (either hosted by the auction site or hosted elsewhere and actively linked) where potential customers can learn more about you, your background, and your specialties. Post a picture of yourself and some of your goods so customers can get a better feel for you.

- Establish a sound and reasonable business policy—customers want to know whether you're organized and if you have a good understanding of how online business should be conducted.

- Whenever possible, discreetly provide hints and teasers about additional merchandise you have available or will be auctioning soon.

AuctionWatch.com has more! _____

For more on this topic, read AW's Attracting a Clientele and Creating an About Me Page tips, at

http://www.auctionwatch.com/awdaily/tipsandtactics/sel-clientele.html

and

http://www.auctionwatch.com/awdaily/tipsandtactics/sel-aboutme.html

If you're curious why this sort of information matters, you should keep in mind that *your* understanding of what you'll sell, why you'll sell it, and who you think will buy it will ultimately drive *how* you'll sell it. Understanding your place in the auction market will help you become more effective when you list your merchandise.

Auction Titles

What's in a title? Everything. A good title needs to be enticing, intriguing, and informative. Since your items will be thrown in the hopper with millions of others, there are certain elements you'll want to include.

What Makes a Good Title?

A good title is specific enough to capture the attention of a targeted group of customers but will also be general enough to attract the curiosity of folks who are just clicking through. Most of all, it should include keywords that a potential shopper will be searching for (such as Topps, Barbie, Tiffany, or any other well-known, desirable, and accurate label). Therefore, a good title should include these elements:

- Use of specific names or brands

- Use of common terms both buyers and browsers will recognize

- Use of associative terms (regarding genre, era, and so on)

- Identification of special attributes (antique, limited edition, promotional, and so on)

- Use of selective capitalization of certain names or words (avoid titles using all caps)

- Concise content but effective use of the maximum number of characters available (usually around 80)

- Proper spelling!

What Makes a Bad Title?

The good news is there are plenty of bad titles out there that will help your good title really stand out. The bad news is you might unwillingly spawn a bad title yourself if you lose sight of your goal to attract as many searchers and lookers as possible by providing as much key information as you can. Bad elements such as these can undermine your efforts:

- Useless appeals such as "L@@K," "awesome," "adorable," "hard-to-find," "rare," and others (an exception would be if you could differentiate your item from other listings by briefly noting condition or scarcity)

- Superfluous use of keyboard characters such as >>>, <<<, !!!!!, ^^^^^, and other meaningless notations

- Deceptive use of words to lure in prospects without actually being associated with such a claim (sometimes known as *keyword spamming*)

- Words that describe a listing element that might be readily visible by other means (such as writing "PIC" when the hosting site posts icons to indicate accompanying pictures)

Keep in mind that the auction description is usually the only opportunity you'll have to attract customers. If you're lazy in composing it, most potential customers will pass it by without a second glance.

AuctionWatch.com has more!

For more on this topic, read AW's Writing Auction Titles tip, at http://www. auctionwatch.com/awdaily/tipsandtactics/index.html

Auction Categories

Choosing categories under which to list your items used to be a simple process. However, since auction sites have become so enormous and category and subcategory headings have become so numerous, choosing the right category now takes some considerable forethought. First, be sure you understand how to choose the proper category for your item:

- Know the categories your customers tend to frequent.

- Choose categories that best identify the items you'll sell and cater to your target audience.

- Whenever possible, avoid general categories.

- Avoid choosing categories unrelated to your item just because you think the category pulls in more traffic. Many buyers are annoyed by sellers who list unrelated items in a category.

Creative Categorizing

Now, if you want to maximize your sales potential (and who doesn't?), then a little out-of-the-box thinking comes in handy. Learn to look at your items a bit differently to see if there's another category or two that might allow you to tap into additional customer pools.

- Recognize crossover appeal of your items (for example, many autographs will also appeal to movie memorabilia collectors and sports memorabilia collectors).

- Identify the deeper subject matter of your items—content or themes that could be properly suited for different categories without appearing out of place.

- Identify subcategories where your customers also search for similar types of items. If appropriate, list under those categories on occasion.

- Broaden your appeal by listing similar items across multiple (appropriate) categories simultaneously. Bidders might check your other auctions and learn about the other categories under which you typically list.

- Try to avoid the very large categories where a plethora of items will tend to bury yours.

Monitor your success rates in certain categories compared to others and adjust future category strategies accordingly.

AuctionWatch.com has more!

For more on this topic, read AW's Choosing Categories tip, at http://www.auctionwatch.com/awdaily/tipsandtactics/sel-categories.html

Auction Descriptions

You've gained a potential bidder's attention with your well-crafted listing title and astute category selection. Now that they're in and ready to check out your merchandise, it's your opportunity to ensure they'll bid. Just like listing titles, auction descriptions can be make-or-break differentiators that show you're an excellent seller—or a clumsy peddler.

What Makes a Good Description?

Remember, you've gotten a customer interested enough to take a deeper look at your merchandise—don't falter now. Here are the attributes of a good description that buyers are hoping to find:

- Get to the point quickly and offer the most salient information up front. It's your hook to help a buyer decide within one or two sentences if your item is the one for which he or she has been searching.

- Provide adequate detail—enough that, if left to words alone, a buyer would be able to form a clear mental picture of your item and its qualities.

- Disclose all imperfections. If you understand your customer base, you should also understand what it is they're looking for or what features matter in the sort of item you're offering.

- Provide information regarding the provenance of the item: where you got it, how long you've owned it, and who owned it before you.

- Provide information regarding any effects the elements have had on the item (such as moisture damage, sun damage, brittleness, or traces of cigarette smoke).

- Don't forget to clearly state or provide a link to your sales policy and be sure to call out any special conditions regarding payment or shipping needs.

- Provide a quick sentence that discreetly informs bidders about other, similar items you might have up for sale.

What Makes a Bad Description?

In many cases, less is more—but not when you're writing an auction description. Your attention to quality and clarity, as well as determining whether *you* would bid on the item based on your description, will help you avoid these common description problems:

- Extremely short or non-edifying descriptions that essentially say only "Here it is and it's $5 extra to ship it."

- Ambiguous language that might leave a bidder wondering whether you're leaving out pertinent information or are attempting some misdirection.

- Errors in spelling and grammar. Always check—a poor job here can be all that's required to drive bidders away.

- Excessive pitch and promotion that doesn't help a bidder assess the actual qualities of the item or your methods of business.

- Subjective statements: "This is the best of its kind and you won't find a better example anywhere" will set most bidders clicking off to other listings.

- Criticisms of other auctions, active or closed, and references to other sellers.

Setting the Hook

Though it's good to get to the point when writing your auction descriptions, there's room for a well-phrased intro. Though you don't want to go overboard with introductory text, a good hook can often help you entice bidders and boost the amounts they consider bidding.

- A hook can be nostalgic in nature, resurrecting old catch phrases or slogans that were used in connection with your item back when it was originally available.

- A hook can also be used to tie your item to current events, trends, or attitudes that might make the item more attractive to today's shopper.

- A hook can be humorous (but not off-color), to connote a feeling of fun or whimsy that might make your item seem more inviting to own.

- A hook can be historic, recounting places or events that help put the bidders in a particular mind-set as they envision the provenance of your item.

- A hook often helps to establish rapport with a potential bidder, especially if it indicates your knowledge of the item.

- A hook is often enough to encourage bidders to read on, eager to know more about your item.

So What's a Good Hook?

Following is one example of an effective introduction:

> *"Looking for that soulful archtop sound that personified the jazz guitar greats of the early '60s, such as Kenny Burrell, Grant Green, and Tal Farlow? Look no further . . . this '56 Gibson ES-175 is a spectacular ax. It's all original and near mint."*

This hook works effectively on several levels:

- It hooks by way of genre (jazz music)

- It hooks by way of association (musicians who have used this style of guitar)

- It hooks by era (recalling the 1960s)

- It hooks by use of recognizable terminology and slang, which develops quick customer rapport ("soulful archtop sound" and "spectacular ax")

It hooks by rapid delivery of interesting information in a few simple sentences.

AuctionWatch.com has more! _____

For more on this topic, read AW's Writing Professional Descriptions tip, at http://www.auctionwatch.com/awdaily/tipsandtactics/sel-descriptions.html

Using HTML for Your Auction Listings

If you're talking up your wares online, it's sometimes more effective when you incorporate the language of the Internet. HTML (*Hypertext Markup Language*) is the resident coding language used across the World Wide Web.

What Can You Do with HTML?

HTML can be incorporated into your auction listings to provide a bit of well-placed pizzazz that will be pleasing to the eye and enticing to your customers.

- You can use special text fonts and sizes to call attention to important information.

- You can use color to add visual appeal and variation to your listings.

- You can present key details using paragraph breaks or bulleted lists.

- You can integrate and place "inline images" (mixed within sections of text).

- You can embed links that can direct a reader to a companion Web page or to larger versions of embedded images.

- You can establish a tone or feel that can psychologically appeal to bidders.

- You can establish a style that many bidders see as an indication of added effort, professionalism, and commitment to business.

How Can HTML Help an Auction Listing?

Of course, too much of anything is bad. When using HTML, moderation is definitely the first order of the day. Before going wild with HTML, know that there are good ways and not-so-good ways to use special visual (and aural) qualities. Below are some of the ways in which HTML can increase the effectiveness of your auction listing:

- It can work as a visual hook through the display of compelling text or an image immediately upon viewing a listing.

- It can visually break up large amounts of text, improving the readability of a listing.

- It can speed up page display by providing embedded links to larger detailed photos or policy text.

- It can stimulate a bidder's interest by making the listing more entertaining and engaging than plain text.

How Can HTML Hurt an Auction Listing?

HTML can be a definite benefit to your auction listings, and can give you an opportunity to truly showcase your wares. However, it can quickly turn into a negative factor, possibly driving away bidders who decide they're not interested in waiting for a bunch of digital gewgaws to load. Following are some of the most common ways HTML can detract from your listing's effectiveness:

- It can easily be overdone, with too many large fonts, blinking text or images, or other needlessly extravagant features.

- It can take too long to display if too many images or animated features are included.

- It can be distracting, forcing potential bidders to slog through excessive decor that can mask the true details of an item.

- It can be annoying, especially when accompanied by music files that can take a long time to load and can be jarring when they finally play.

AuctionWatch.com has more!

For more on this topic, read AW's Learning HTML tip, at http://www.auctionwatch.com/awdaily/tipsandtactics/sel-html.html

Auction Photos

Though you may decide that a simple approach to listing items suits you, one thing you should definitely consider is the inclusion of photos, usually referred to as *images*. It can't be said too often: images can make the difference between successful and unsuccessful auction listings—bidders often won't bid without them.

Why are photos so important to bidders? Here are the simple reasons:

- Images allow a bidder to inspect the item visually prior to committing to bid.

- Images provide a much-needed reference for identification and authentication.

- Images allow bidders to compare a visual representation of an item with the written description provided, highlighting any possible discrepancies or misrepresentations.

- Images can provide close-up views of an item so the bidder can review critical detail and physical attributes.

- Images allow bidders to learn more about the items they're interested in, often offering the first glimpse of an item once heard of but never seen.

- Images can reduce the need for a bidder to contact a seller to ask additional questions (though they can often give rise to more questions as well).

But including images means more work for the seller. What, then, do sellers have to gain by going the extra yard to provide images in their auctions?

- Images allow sellers to visually showcase their items.

- Images are often the key to getting a bidder to bid, even a bidder that wasn't truly interested in the item (that is, before taking a look at the image and becoming hooked).

- Images are an easy way of providing full disclosure of an item's condition or completeness, which is often indispensable for straightening out post-auction disputes or misunderstandings.

- Images can augment descriptive text enormously, and can often communicate more effectively than paragraphs of written details.

Many buyers flatly refuse to bid on an auction item that doesn't have accompanying images; they will not buy sight-unseen.

Integrating Photos into Your Listings

Once you are convinced that images are going to be a regular feature in your auctions, consider how you'll acquire those precious pictures. The good news is there are several ways to get your pictures online and in front of your customers.

Get a Digital Camera

The most direct method is to purchase a digital camera of your own (or win one at an auction site). Owning your own camera gives you the freedom to take pictures whenever you need them and to upload them to your PC (and later the Internet) with incredible ease. If you held off on getting a digital camera while you were setting up your auction office, think it over again now.

Get a Digital Scanner

The alternative is to get a scanner (also on your office equipment checklist), which is typically less expensive than a camera. Remember that scanners are usually best for smaller, flat objects.

Develop Your 35mm Film to Digital Files

Most film processing firms offer digital developing, and deliver a 3.5" floppy disk or Photo CD containing all of your images. The cost of such processing is typically comparable to regular print processing. Many firms provide digital development on the Internet, which allows you to view and download pictures taken with your conventional camera.

Borrow Equipment or Ask a Friend

If you're not sure you want to invest in any equipment, find a friend who already has the hardware and ask for his assistance. You'll quickly learn that this equipment will pay for itself in no time, and you'll have the opportunity to try out a camera or scanner before you make a purchase of your own.

 **AuctionWatch.com has more!**

If you want to learn how to determine which digital camera or scanner is for you and which features are worth the money you'll spend, see these AW feature articles:

Picture Perfect: Digital Camera Roundup, at

http://www.auctionwatch.com/awdaily/features/digitalcamera/index.html

Going Digital: Digital Scanner Roundup, at

http://www.auctionwatch.com/awdaily/features/scanner/index.html

Editing Your Images

Assuming you now have your images, you'll need to quickly determine if they need any touching up. Use any of the commercially available (and often free trial downloadable) image editors such as PaintShop Pro, LviewPro, or Microsoft Picture-It to make a few necessary adjustments to better represent what you're selling. Specifically, you'll want to do some simple editing in these situations:

- Your images are excessively bright, dark, or oversaturated with color.

- Your images do not properly represent your item. (Digital images can sometimes make an item appear better than it truly is and you'll want to adjust color or contrast to be sure that what you see on the screen is what your eventual customer will hold in his or her hands.)

- Your images require cropping to remove any unnecessary or distracting elements—other items, furniture, people, pets, or whatever.

- Your images require resizing to make them load faster in an auction listing. (Take care in this step and double-check the results—it's easy to damage image quality when you resize the file.)

You wish to incorporate several images in a collage-style presentation that will work effectively within your listing.

AuctionWatch.com has more!

For more on this topic see AW's Touching Up Photos tip, at http://www. auctionwatch.com/awdaily/tipsandtactics/sel-touchup.html

Once your images are ready for show, you'll need to upload them to the Internet. The most direct method is to use AuctionWatch.com's free Image Hosting service. The Image Hosting tool makes it easy to upload your images from your PC (or external storage device), store and manage them online, and link them to your auction for its duration. Check out the additional details and features of Image Hosting in the AuctionWatch.com Auction Manager area.

Pulling It All Together

Next, when it's time to review a listing, give it the once-over to be sure it represents your item (and *you*) in the best way possible:

- Check for proper spelling and grammar.

- Check completeness and accuracy of information provided.

- Check that all images are showing up properly and as intended.

- Check that any and all HTML code is functioning properly.

- Check your selection of auction duration, opening bid amount, and other details required by the host site (more on taming these aspects in Chapter 8, "Sharpening Your Sales Skills").

- Check how fast your auction listing loads; make content adjustments (images or HTML) if it takes longer than 10 seconds for content to appear.

- Check how appealing the information is to you. If you were a bidder, would you be enticed to bid? (If not, figure out why and make adjustments.)

Key Watch Points

- **To list effectively, you'll need to understand the sorts of items you intend to sell and how you intend to present yourself (and your business) in the process of selling.**

- **Determine who your target customers are, what their wants and needs are, and how you can best solicit their business through effective listing.**

- **Develop a knack for crafting effective and enticing auction titles, and be sure to include many of the keywords for which your customers might be likely to search.**

- **Be sure your descriptions are informative, accurate, honest, and even entertaining in order to convince potential bidders that you are the best seller with whom to do business.**

- **Give your bidders more in the way of images and effective HTML enhancements, but be sure your listings don't become excessively showy or slow to display.**

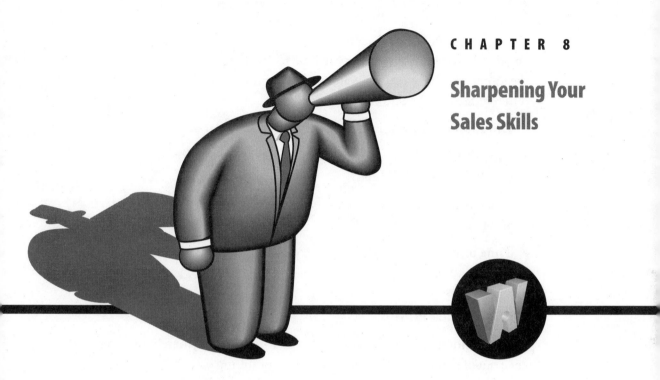

CHAPTER 8

Sharpening Your Sales Skills

Level:	**Intermediate**
Reader:	**Seller**

Now it's time to dig deeper and really start developing your sales savvy. Once you master the nuances of selling at online auctions, you will really separate yourself from much of the competition while improving the return on your investment. These aren't difficult skills or concepts—in fact, many are based on simple logic and common sense. However, many of the easiest paths to success are often overlooked. Stop, then, and consider these additional keys to your success, and make them a part of your auction know-how.

Timing Your Auctions

The great thing about the Internet and online auctions is that they're open 24 hours a day, 7 days a week, 365 days a year. You can shop or sell any time of any day. However, if it's selling you'll be focused on, you'll want to watch for the times that are best for your business. From a high level, consider the different factors of auction timing.

- **Duration of the auction**. how many days will your auction run?

- **Day of the week**. what day of the week will your auction start and what day of the week will it end?

- **Time of the day**. what time of the day or night will your auction start and (more important) end?

- **Time of the year**. will the month (or the season) make any difference to your auction?

Is It All in the Timing?

If you wonder whether fretting over auction timing is merely making science out of simplicity, consider the impact of timing on each of these factors (and vice versa):

- **Peak potential**. although they have 24/7 access to the auctions, most people don't use it. There are times when lots of people are apt to be online and visiting auctions and times when it's much less active in the online salesrooms.

- **Bidder activity**. there are specific times of the day, days of the week, and weeks of the year when bidding will be most active (and when it will diminish).

- **Site activity**. hosting sites tend to bog down at certain times. They also usually schedule regular downtime for maintenance.

- **Your personal timetable**. you probably don't function equally well round the clock either—consider the times when *you* can and cannot stage and manage auctions.

Now, consider the proven times when auction activity is at a high and at a low, and plan each into your listing strategy.

Auction Duration

Auctions can run for different periods of time. Here are the most common types—and how each can help or hurt your final results:

- **3-day auctions**. Great for quick sales and for capitalizing on upcoming events (such as holidays); eager buyers like the shortened cycle to improve their chances of winning or getting a bargain; many 3-day auctions happen so quickly they come and go without being seen by the larger bidding population.

- **5-day auctions**. A better choice for attracting more potential "views" from bidders; still short enough to entice the impatient; decent turnaround for a relatively quick sale; still has potential to end before all potential bidders can discover it.

- **7-day auctions**. Perhaps the best and most widely chosen duration among sellers; attracts more bidders since it can span an entire week (weekend-to-weekend) of viewing activity; still a reasonable length for a rapid sell (or buy).

- **10-day auctions**. In a word, long; spans two weekends to draw bidders; possibly preferable during holiday periods; may lose bidders, though, who aren't interested in waiting so long or potentially enduring the additional bidding competition.

- **14-day auctions**. Too long; good for spanning major holidays, but not much else.

Starting and Ending Day of the Week

What a difference a day makes! Experienced sellers are very deliberate in choosing which day their auctions will start and, more important, which day of the week they will end.

- **On a weekend**. Probably the best choice since most of the workforce has weekends off. It's debatable whether Saturday or Sunday is a better day for bidder activity—both days are quite active. Be sure to coordinate the start date of 3-day or 5-day auctions to ensure a weekend end day.

- **On a weekday**. Still plenty of activity on weekdays but definitely not as active as weekends due to folks' regular work schedules. Not bad, though, for working around a holiday or if you intend to consistently have auctions starting and ending throughout each week.

Starting and Ending Times of the Day

The start and end times of an auction are perhaps the most crucial considerations. By and large, the best time to start or end an auction will be in the evening hours—folks are typically better able to browse for extended periods of time and can be more available to bid in an auction's final minutes. Consider time zones, though, and try to allow West Coast citizens time to get home from work without making East Coast citizens stay up all night. (Hint: between 6 P.M. and 8 P.M. Pacific Time is the usual choice.)

AuctionWatch.com has more!

Learn more about timing your auctions in AW's comprehensive Tips & Tactics section at http://www.auctionwatch.com/awdaily/tipsandtactics/sel-time.html

Be sure to consider your bidding audience when deciding on ending times of several auctions you will run, especially those that feature similar or related items. Allow at least five minutes between auction endings to give a bidder the opportunity to monitor multiple auctions without having to miss out on any due to simultaneous closing times.

Time of the Year

Take note of the different seasons, not only as opportunities to feature seasonal items, but also to account for times when many people will be away from their PCs (such as on holidays). Avoid closing auctions directly on a holiday—many people aren't online.

To sum up, when timing an auction always take your customers' surfing and bidding habits into account. Many sellers have reported receiving kudos from their customers for running auctions that are easy to bid on, thanks to customer-considerate timing.

Service Highlight

The best way to keep a fresh understanding of trends in bidding activity is to employ the use of AuctionWatch.com counters. Counters can be added to any auction listing and will track the number of "views" your item receives. More important, the AW counter service also provides you with statistical data that reveals *when* most of the views occurred—that's the data you'll want to incorporate to better adjust the optimal timing for your auction starts and stops. You'll find AW counters in the *Auction Manager* section of AuctionWatch.com.

Recognizing and Responding to Trends

Whether they're looking at a traditional cultural celebration, a historic event, or the effect of today's current hype, savvy sellers learn to recognize, respond to, and anticipate special occasions and situations in which certain merchandise will attract more bidders and higher bids.

Holidays

There's always opportunity to bolster your sales in conjunction with major (and minor) holidays. Even though ending an auction on a holiday isn't the best for business, it's useful to position your auctions to feature holiday-related items (Halloween and Christmas items are always big favorites) or to feature items that folks might want or need *before* the big holiday arrives.

Annual Events

Don't forget to take note of other cultural and media happenings that can bring more bids for your items by capitalizing on people's anticipation of the big event. Consider positioning items to sell in conjunction with the Academy Awards, Grammy Awards, special exhibits, tours, or reunions.

AuctionWatch.com has more!

Check out AW's extensive seller tips Selling for the Holidays and Selling Strategies for Spring Cleaning at

http://www.auctionwatch.com/awdaily/tipsandtactics/sel-holiday.html

and

http://www.auctionwatch.com/awdaily/tipsandtactics/sel-clean.html

Historic Events

Think about how events like elections, space exploration missions, and even technological incidents (remember Y2K?) can work to bring more attention and timeliness to your auctions.

Fads and Frenzies

All of the big manufacturers are seated firmly on the latest bandwagon—why shouldn't you climb on? Marketers are working hard and spending hard to usher in the next craze. To you, that means selling items that are in line with what the masses are clamoring for. This is especially pertinent in this time of nostalgia: reissues are hot business today, and that makes original items hotter still. Also, short-supply, high-demand new items are terrific to resell when you can get your hands on them (think of Furbies, Beanie Babies, Pokemon cards, and all those other "gotta have it" goods).

Service Highlight

Monitor the crazes before you list a related item. Use AW's Universal Search in conjunction with Track Auction in Auction Manager. Simply perform a search, select the results in which you are interested, and monitor their bidding activity within Auction Manager. Learn more at http://www.auctionwatch. com/help/acp/myawfaq.html

Generational Cycles

Think about the nostalgia you feel for particular items. You grew up with them; they remind you of the good times gone by. Then, look to the next generation of younger people and consider the items those folks will want to recapture.

Your key to success in harnessing the sales power of trends is to anticipate the trend and to sell when demand is nearest its peak. If you're too early, the hype will not have reached full tilt. If you're too late, you're just another one trying to sell that thing that fell out of vogue last month.

AuctionWatch.com has more! _____

Identify trends before they happen; see AW's extensive seller tip on Buying for Resale at http://www.auctionwatch.com/help/acp/myawfaq.html

The Price That Entices

People really will often pass over a $20 item but buy it at $19.99, so you'll want to employ a bit of price positioning and a little psychology to bring in the bidders. Your intent is not to mislead or manipulate bidders. Rather, you'll be using your understanding of the market paired with your personal sales needs to develop a pricing strategy that brings in more sales with fewer missed opportunities.

First, establish an understanding of the potential selling price your item might command:

- Review other auctions for the same item and determine the average selling price.

- Determine the demand for your item. Are all auctions for similar items receiving lots of bids and resulting in high final sales prices?

- Determine the supply of your item. How many others are for sale right now and in the recent past?

- Determine if the item is time-sensitive (seasonal demand, limited supply, fleeting popularity).

- Consider the condition and completeness of your item. Damage, wear, or lost parts can reduce the value of an item by half or more.

- Identify your sales goal—a rapid sale at a lower profit or a slower sale at a higher profit? Translated: can you wait to land that target price or would you be you better served by lowering your expectations slightly to make the sure sale?

- Consider the least amount you'd be willing to accept for your item.

- Be realistic; beware of falling into the trap of going for the big bucks with *every* auction—bidders will pass you by if your wares are always too rich.

- Consider what *you'd* pay for the item—that often determines what others might pay for it.

With your goals and expectations clear, you can properly price your items. The trick is to price them in a way that draws in bidders and draws in profit.

Low Minimum Bids

Sometimes, a ridiculously low starting price can be the beginning of a very lucrative auction. Here's why low minimum bids are effective:

- Bidders love bargains and most will bid a dollar or two without much thought just for the chance to get a great deal.

- Bidders hate to lose. That casual first bid is often enough to get somebody emotionally involved in the auction—and inclined to bid further when the competition heats up.

- Low minimum bids encourage bidders to "play," inciting activity for the auction and excitement to see how cheaply an item can be had.

- Low minimum bids don't necessarily mean you'll take a loss on the item. An item will typically realize its market value by the time the auction has ended.

So should every auction feature a low minimum bid? Consider these situations when the low opening price is *not* the best approach:

- To some buyers, a low opening bid might indicate a lesser quality item—else why would you be offering it so cheap?

- Some hard-core bargain hunters, known as "bottom feeders," scour auctions for ridiculous deals and bid on everything and anything that's cheap. Some lose track of their numerous bids and sellers tell of bidders who get great deals but fail to follow through with payment.

High Minimum Bids

If you know what it's worth, why not avoid the lowball game and price it at the market value? Sometimes that's not a bad idea. Here's when this strategy can work in your favor:

- Higher price often communicates higher quality. Your confidence in using a higher starting bid, when justified with a high-quality or highly desirable piece, lets bidders know you're serious about delivering an exceptional item.

- Higher price effectively weeds out the bottom feeders and other auction "gamers" (those who bid for the fun of it), leaving you with a group of bidders who are serious about purchasing your item.

- Higher price indicates you're knowledgeable about your item, provided you *are* and demonstrate your knowledge in your assessment of the item, its description, and the images you provide.

Of course, the higher starting bid has drawbacks:

- High starting bids often stall initial bid activity; remember that everyone's looking for a chance at a bargain.

- High starting bids sometimes weed out *too many* bidders, effectively cutting off the benefit of having multiple bidders bidding against one another.

- High starting bids cause some bidders to think the seller is greedy or uninformed about the item.

Reserve Prices

Reserve prices sound like (and often are) a good precaution—but bear in mind that most bidders don't care much for them. Why? To many bidders, a reserve price is a "fixed" price; they contend that sellers should simply use the reserve as their minimum bid price if they care that much about getting it. The best bet is to use reserve prices sparingly, allowing the natural work of the auction market to determine the value of your items. Use reserve prices all the time and you'll develop a reputation as a "fixed price seller." But you can use reserve prices effectively when the following factors are especially important to you:

- Reserve prices allow a low starting bid, encouraging initial bidding activity.

- Reserve prices protect a seller's investment or belief of the value of an item. They make sure you either receive a price you can live with or keep the item—perhaps for a later and more successful auction.

- Reserve prices, like high minimum bid prices, can effectively deter the less-serious auction gamer.

Expect to spend a certain amount of time "experimenting" with your auctions. Determine which items match up best to the different pricing options. If an item doesn't sell, reconsider your pricing strategy and, without taking a loss, make adjustments to get the bidders to notice and bid on your item.

AuctionWatch.com has more!

Entice those prospective buyers! See AW's extensive seller tip Encouraging Bids, at http://www.auctionwatch.com/awdaily/tipsandtactics/sel-encouragingbids.html

Keys to Item Grading

The best sellers understand that proper grading can better assure good prices and happy customers. However, grading is one of the grayest areas of selling at online auctions. The problem is that grading is a very subjective matter. It's entirely possible for the seller to think an item looks like it just came off a store shelf while the buyer thinks it looks more like it just fell off a truck.

Why Should the Words You Choose Matter?

The first thing to consider is why grading eludes the "rose by any other name" adage:

- There are no universally accepted grading definitions. Items—such as furniture, stamps, glassware, and trading cards—are often described using terms specific to the kind of item in question.

- Acceptance of a stated grade usually depends on the experience of a buyer or seller. A new buyer is probably more willing to accept a seller's grade of an item, whereas a more experienced buyer (often buying to "upgrade" an existing piece) may be concerned with every detail and imperfection.

- Some sellers consider the age of an item—especially if it can be called antique—as being a positive influence on the grading. ("It's in excellent condition *for its age*." Warning! Warning!)

- Too often sellers rely on merely stating a grade without providing a detailed description of the item that supports the grade. Without details, buyers can't tell if the grade is accurate.

So What's the Terminology?

Though they're not universally used, here are the generally accepted terms for most items being sold:

- **Mint**. It is "as new," without any damage or defects. Abbreviated as *MT*. Also look for *Mint In Box* (*MIB*), *Mint In Sealed Box* (*MISB*), *Mint On Card* (*MOC*), *Mint In Package* (*MIP*), and other variations.

- **Near Mint**. "Like new" with perhaps a single (or very few) minor defects or damaged areas. Abbreviated as *NM* and possibly in conjunction with other abbreviations used for Mint (for example, *NMIB*).

- **Very Fine**. A few more small drawbacks or just one significant enough to prevent it from being termed at a higher grade. Abbreviated as *VF*.

- **Fine**. A desirable condition but with more noticeable shortcomings. Abbreviated as *FN*.

- **Very Good**. A decent piece but one that shows more visible wear or handling, or suffers from minor incompleteness. Abbreviated as *VG*.

- **Good**. It clearly shows wear, use, or damage. It's OK to own, but probably not the end-all piece in terms of condition. Abbreviated as *GD*.

- **Fair**. Probably suffering from more significant damage or use. Most likely has unsightly visible defects and is incomplete. Rarely abbreviated.

- **Poor**. It's trash, period. Anybody want it, for free perhaps?

How Do You Decide on a Grade?

Of course, you'll need to become familiar with the items you'll sell to determine if the enthusiasts use any specialized terms not mentioned here. When it comes to deciding on an accurate grade for your item, use these guiding points to select the fairest assessment:

- **Be objective**. For the moment, forget what you have invested in the item.

- **Be fair**. If it's only in *Good* condition, don't try to talk it up or conveniently "overlook" an imperfection in order to improve the grade.

- **Beware**. Buyers are quite particular and any overzealous grading might result in returns from dissatisfied buyers. If your grading is consistently inaccurate, you'll develop a reputation that will precede you on every auction.

How Do You Describe the Grade You Assign?

So, when it comes time to list your item, include your assessment of the grade in the following manner:

- Use the recognized grading terms. Don't confuse bidders with fabricated terms like "super condition," "really nice," and "great specimen." Avoidance of accepted terms will make you appear inexperienced or potentially dishonest.

- Accompany the grade with a full disclosure of the item's details. Help the bidder decide if your assessment of the item seems reasonable.

- Consider using "half-grades" (Very Fine +, Near Mint -) if you're on the fence about where the item truly grades out.

- Consider carefully *under*grading your item. Without taking too much away from the item, let bidders know you're using a harsh grading system and grade down a half step. This usually results in feedback from buyers proclaiming your items arrive "better than described"—which is the kind of good PR you want!

- Be sure you match your minimum bid price or reserve price to the grade you select. A noticeable mismatch will not sit well with bidders.

- Invite questions about your grading methods and any additional details a bidder may require.

AuctionWatch.com has more!

Read AW's extensive seller tip Declaring Accurate Grades, at http://www.auctionwatch.com/awdaily/tipsandtactics/sel-grade.html

The Importance of Item Expertise

With all that's been written here, you might think you need to become an expert if you're going to really get ahead at the auctions. Well, it helps. Actually, buyers are looking for experts when they look around at the auctions. Here's why your expertise is important—not only to you but to your buyers as well:

- Being an expert in what you sell will give you confidence in *how* you'll sell and at what prices.

- Being an expert helps you find your customers and better understand their wants and needs.

- Being an expert helps you write better item descriptions and present better images that show your buyers the critical views.

- Being an expert helps you anticipate changes in demand, supply, and your customers' expectations.

- Being an expert helps you fend off dishonest buyers (as well as dishonest sellers)—you're armed with the facts and knowledge you need to avoid a scam.

- Being an expert gains you the respect and repeat business of your customers, those who realize that you know your stuff.

How Do You Become an Expert?

It's definitely not something to be achieved overnight, but here's what you can do to build your expertise in a way that will keep you on top of your game, in touch with your market, and in high demand with your customers:

- Become intimately familiar with your chosen area. Learn the look, feel, smell, and even taste (if practical) of the items in your area of expertise. Discerning buyers use as many of their senses as possible (in addition to common sense) to identify and differentiate the items they seek.

- Know the history of your items, individually as well as collectively. Understand the history of the item maker, from where these items originally hailed, and where they can be found today.

- Understand variations implicitly. Know the evolution of your item, if "errors" were produced, and what key details help you pinpoint the exact time frame and situation of the item at hand.

- Learn to recognize reproductions. Whether you're looking at a licensed reissue or reproduction or an outright fake, you need to be able to quickly identify a nonauthentic piece.

- Learn who the other experts are and seek them out. Many people hunt down the experts as sources of additional information and validation.

- Visit shows and exhibits where you can see more of the items you specialize in but might not presently own. Talk to expert dealers and salespeople about the items, picking up more details about origin, value, and market demand.

- Read! Build a reference library of books, magazines, Internet articles, and whatever else contains facts, figures, and photos of the items you specialize in.

- Join groups, clubs, and societies that specialize in your item and develop a network of regular information sharing.

A healthy passion for expertise makes research and learning fun, but developing expertise still takes time. And, for all of your efforts, how will you communicate that you're an expert? Actually, you don't need to in so many words. Be informed, articulate, and open to inquiries and your customers (and other sellers) will quickly learn that you know what you're talking about.

AuctionWatch.com has more!

Don't miss AW's weekly market reports from recognized experts in collectibles, decorative arts, and fine art, available in AW's Collector's Beat area at http://www.auctionwatch.com/collectors/

Standing Out in the Crowd

You're a sharp seller and your items are terrific. Still, the truth is that yours is one of millions of items available at the auction. How can you make sure your item will get noticed? Well, there's no sure-fire method to guarantee you'll climb above the masses—but what you've just learned will help. Here are a few more tidbits to help set yourself apart from all of the rest:

- Be professional in all your business dealings, from your high-quality auction descriptions all the way through to executing a smooth final transaction.

- Be helpful to all customers and potential customers. Show your commitment to your business by showing your commitment to your customers.

- Be reasonable in all of your transactions. Develop and deliver a sales policy that makes dealing with you easy and problem-free.

- Provide the right kinds of items at the right times at the right price. Customers will know you're offering what they want and know you have a sane method for putting the goods up on the auction block.

- Go the extra yard for your customers. Simple things like sending follow-up e-mail after a sale, including handwritten "thank you" notes with the items you ship, and employing cost-reducing methods that help you pass the savings on to those who buy from you. Customers will recognize even the littlest perks and will remember you the next time they come bidding.

- Be an expert. Know your stuff and your customers will remember you.

- Be friendly. Enjoy your work, appreciate your customers, and have fun at what you do. Your customers will enjoy dealing with you when they sense you enjoy dealing with them.

Though it all sounds a bit too rosy, these extras can be just what customers are hoping to encounter, even though they may not realize it themselves. Never underestimate the power of the conveyance of an online smile and a pleasant disposition.

Bulk Listing Tools and Techniques

One way to gain more results with less effort is to use a bulk listing tool—an application that allows you to generate, queue up, and launch many auctions at the same time. Anyone can list one item at a time, but the truly effective sellers are putting out listings en masse and getting more done for it.

Serious sellers are turning to bulk listing applications, such as AW's Auction Manager Pro (available for download at http://www.auctionwatch.com/my/client/), for these compelling reasons:

- Bulk listings can be created offline, without need to log on to the Internet, allowing you to freely create a collection of listings while you're on the go (perhaps using a laptop).

- Bulk listings can be assembled at your pace, allowing you to upload the entire collection of items whenever you're ready.

- Bulk listings can be queued up for several auction sites and launched whenever you're ready. In fact, Auction Manager Pro enables merchants to schedule the posting of their listings. Then, their listings will launch while they are offline.

- Using bulk listers helps you reduce the amount of time you spend listing, freeing you up to spend more time on other aspects of your business.

Making the Most of Bulk Listers

To get the best final result when using bulk listers, keep the following points in mind:

- List similar items so that bidders will see several related objects you have up for bid concurrently; at other times, it's better to list a potpourri of items so you'll be sure to offer something for everyone.

- List your items so they'll be active and will end at times of peak bidding.

- Bulk listers, such as Auction Manager Pro, will start all of your auctions at precisely the same time (or within a few seconds), which translates to synchronized ending times.

- Choose a day (or days) when you'll upload and release your bulk listings. Work your other activities around those days so you'll be sure to spend as much or more time tending to the rest of your business.

- Keep the site's listing fees in mind and anticipate the total fee for the number of items you'll launch.

- When all those auctions end, you'll be in a flurry of sending out payment notifications as well as packing and shipping merchandise. Be sure to factor that impact on your workload and stagger your listing days so you won't be caught having to do too much at double-time.

Cross-Sell on Multiple Sites in Multiple Formats

It's typical that many auction-goers, both buyers and sellers, will settle into a favorite auction site. That's not a bad thing—working the same site enables a seller to become extremely familiar with the site's functions, its clientele, and the overall attitude shared among the membership. However, don't overlook the power of "divide and conquer:" by breaking out of the auction comfort zone, sellers can often find new populations of customers eager to be served.

- Analyze the different items being offered at the different sites. Compare prices for similar items to determine if your chosen site seems to be the *best* site to sell a particular type of goods.

- If an item doesn't sell at one site, re-list it at a different site to see how well it will fare there.

- List similar (or identical) items simultaneously at different sites and compare the final results.

- Compare site fees versus final values to see where you can gain the better profit after listing expenses and commissions have been deducted.

- Besides listing at different sites, list using different formats. If you have multiple units of an item, compare how a single-item auction does versus a Dutch auction. Learn how the bidders tend to gravitate toward one format or the other. Further, if you have inventory of a specific item, consider single auctions initially, then list the rest "Dutch" when the market price stabilizes.

AuctionWatch.com has more!

Learn what distinguishes one auction site from the next in AW's extensive buyer and seller tip Evaluating Sites, at http://www.auctionwatch.com/awdaily/ tipsandtactics/buy-evaluating.html

Granted, it will take more effort to manage auctions across different sites, but there's no better way to determine how the sites' markets are evolving (or eroding) if you don't manage at least a few side-by-side comparisons occasionally.

Keys to Re-Listing

If you're discouraged when your item doesn't sell (either no bids or reserve price not met), don't lose hope. Thousands of auctions end the same way. The auction sites don't want to see disappointed auctioneers lose interest, so they have worked to develop convenient ways to facilitate re-listing an item.

Of course, there are no real "secrets" to re-listing an item, but there are approaches you can take that reduce your time to put an item up for a second or third go-round and strategies to use that might help you better ensure your success on a re-listing venture.

- Understand the site's re-listing process. Can you click a link to quickly relaunch your auction? Does the site have an automatic re-listing feature that executes if your auction ends without a successful winning bid?

- Understand the site's fee structure and if you'll be charged listing fees for items that don't sell, as well as re-listing fees if you decide to give it another shot.

- Determine if, as you re-list, you're able to change information in your listing without having your auction considered a "new" item as opposed to merely a re-list.

- Does the site limit the number of times you can re-list, fee or no fee?

If at First You Don't Succeed...

After you understand the site's mechanics and conditions in re-listing, pause and take some time to learn from the unsuccessful auction. Perhaps you need a change in approach and strategy as you prepare to re-list:

- Review your auction title for clarity and maximum "hit" keywords (for buyers' searches).

- Review your auction category and determine if it was the best choice, the only choice, or if there's a better choice available.

- Review your auction description to be sure it's informative, accurate, and engaging.

- Did you offer images of the item?

- Was your minimum bid price or reserve price set too high? Can you adjust it down or forgo the reserve and trust the bidders to bring you a reasonable price?

- Was this the best time to list? Review the time, day, and season of your auction and determine if an adjustment is in order.

- Did you list at the best site? Might you do better by listing this item at a different site?

- How many times have you re-listed (if this isn't just your second go-round)? Is it possible there's simply no interest in your item at this time?

There is a value in a failed auction: it communicates that your approach, somehow and somewhere, didn't quite work. Be very open, perceptive, and flexible with each of your auctions. In many cases, it's a fine-tuning procedure where you're stabilizing your business approach and adjusting your offerings. Re-listings allow you to "tinker" with your process until you can lock into your customer base in a way that has you bringing in the bids every time.

AuctionWatch.com has more!

Learn more selling techniques; see AW's extensive seller tip Relisting Auctions, at http://www.auctionwatch.com/awdaily/tipsandtactics/sel-relist.html

Key Watch Points

- Recognize the subtleties of listing items for sale by mastering the finer points of selling at auctions.

- Learn how to analyze the auction market to determine the best ways to time, present, and price your auctions.

- Identify your customer pool and identify their likes, dislikes, wants, and needs when it comes to bidding on and buying at the auctions.

- Introduce special elements into your auction listings to make them more informative and attractive, but stop short of making them excessively decorated or distracting.

- Grade your items fairly and accurately, and then knock them down a half-grade so your customers will always get an item that's better than they expect.

- Become an expert in the items you'll sell and customers will seek you out as a knowledgeable and trusted seller.

- Learn to adjust your listing strategies and use a variety of sites, formats, and bulk listing techniques to improve your profit potential while reducing your labor time.

CHAPTER 9

Understanding Copyrighted, Infringing, and Forbidden Items

Level: *Intermediate*

Reader: *Buyer and Seller*

The auction block is crowded with stuff—things that are clutter in one place but treasure in another; things one person can get in quantity that another can't find at all; things someone got for free but knows other folks are willing to pay for—all perfect situations for pulling in profit. However, is it *legal* to buy and sell all this stuff? Unfortunately, not all of it is. Some of the material and content on the block may legally belong to someone other than the seller. And some of it may fall into categories of items that the auction sites have forbidden for sale. You should carefully consider all of this before you buy *or* sell, especially since online auction sites have grown into bona fide businesses complete with assorted legal authorities watching over them. It's important for you to understand whether the deal will boil down to ill-gotten goods or gain.

What the Sites Forbid

For starters, all auction sites have clearly posted what they call "forbidden items." Simply put, if you attempt to sell this stuff, your auctions will be shut down, you could be subject to revocation of your registered status, and you could possibly even face prosecution. Yikes!

So what's forbidden? Well, that could vary from site to site, but there *is* a group of usual suspects.

Alcohol

Alcohol is generally forbidden for auction because of the complex taxation, import, and licensing rules that cover it. Unless you're bidding at a licensed site and dealing with sellers licensed to deal in alcohol (such as at a site like Winebid.com), the rules generally state that alcohol auctions will be promptly closed by the site.

Firearms

Though firearms are sometimes considered a sort of collectible (for period pieces), most sites now forbid auctioning of any mechanism originally designed to fire some sort of projectile. There are, however, some sites that are properly licensed and specialize in auctioning such items—see ArmsAuction.com, for example, if this is a field you want to get into.

Fireworks

These are illegal in many states and other parts of the world. They are, therefore, not eligible for auctioning.

Drugs and Drug Paraphernalia

These are illegal goods, plain and simple.

Human Parts and Remains

Yuck. However, at eBay, the rules do state that selling skulls and skeletons for educational purposes is allowed.

Live Animals

Unless you've made a warehouse find of vintage Sea Monkeys, dealing with the sale and shipping of live animals is typically left to the pros (animal handlers and such). Since the potential for trouble is so high (from critters arriving DOA or delivery trucks harboring "funny odors"), auction sites have taken the safe route and barred such auctions.

Stolen or Counterfeit Goods

They're stolen. They're illegal. They aren't allowed for auctioning. 'Nuff said.

Some sites have even more limitations, including disclosure of *questionable items* and *infringing items*. If you're a seller, it's your duty to understand the site's rules about items listed for auction and to make sure the items you sell aren't illegal, infringing, or unnatural—in other words, forbidden. And as a buyer you're best served if you avoid forbidden items, since many are discovered and summarily removed from the auction site—bids or no bids.

Why They Forbid 'Em

But why are these sorts of items forbidden? Well, aside from some of the obvious reasons (like illegality), auction sites also state these reasons:

- Since P2P sites never actually possess the goods for sale, they are unable to verify the legality or appropriateness of questionable or potentially infringing goods.

- Many goods that might be sold are subject to local statutes that differ from state to state and country to country.

- For health, environmental, and agricultural reasons, some goods will violate import or export statutes.

- In some cases, sites might actually be subject to liability for the sale and subsequent effects of certain goods.

Deals, Steals, and Gray Market Goods

Doggone, this stuff is great and it's cheap, too! But wait—is it legal? Certain items are perennial favorites of backroom sellers; you might be unpleasantly surprised to find that you're bidding on illicit goods. What are the usual kinds of things that come from these dens of thieves? Following are the most common:

- Computer software

- Electronics (small and mid-sized)

- Music (CDs and cassettes)

- Movies (VHS and DVD)

- Pornographic material (though not necessarily stolen, often the content of some of it is illegal)

- Knock-offs (illegal copies of name-brand items)

- Printed matter (undisclosed copies or restrikes)

More bad merchandise exists than you'd probably care to imagine, but these tend to be the most common, largely due to their relative ease of handling as well as their profit potential.

Let the Buyer Be Aware

As a buyer, it's up to you to sniff out the rat and quickly identify items that might be bogus or stolen. When you search the auctions for items to bid on, do a little research to make sure everything's on the up-and-up:

- Check the seller's feedback rating first! Are there any comments that might indicate trouble?

- Compare the potential selling price of the item to what the market usually bears; if it's *too* cheap, remember the old saying about things too good to be true.

- Pay close attention to the item's description and determine if any key information has been omitted. Is the description blatantly incorrect in terms of the item being described? Is the description evasive in a way that makes you wonder if the auction's on the level?

- Contact the seller to ask questions. If you don't receive a reply or receive a very curt and uninformative reply, think twice about bidding. (If nothing else, this could simply indicate a seller who might not be very responsive and might not manage the post-auction activity to your liking.)

- Study the seller's policy: does it contain harsh or potentially unreasonable terms (short payment period, no returns or guarantees)—and no good explanation for the policy? Does the seller seem to be in an unusual hurry to sell and wrap up business?

Most importantly, be knowledgeable about the items you might bid on and be able to determine signs of stolen or illegally reproduced material. It's not such a good deal if you end up with merchandise that isn't even worth the "bargain" price you paid.

AuctionWatch.com has more!

See AW's extensive buyer tip Identifying Questionable Auctions, at http://www. auctionwatch.com/awdaily/tipsandtactics/buy-identify.html

Also, don't miss our feature "Materially Different: Online Auction Misrepresentation," at http://www.auctionwatch.com/awdaily/features/materially/index.html

The A-B-Cs of Copyright

Copyright is usually a gray area in the minds of folks who buy and sell stuff, at online auctions and elsewhere—items change hands regularly, someone knows someone who can get a rare pressing or reproduction of a work, someone happened to be standing by as a bunch of licensed material was being discarded, and so on. Whether it's music, software, promotional materials, or similar items, copyright can become an issue more often than most people realize.

The official definition of copyright as presented by the U.S. Copyright Office goes like this:

"Copyright is a form of protection provided by the laws of the United States (Title 17, U.S. Code) to the authors of 'original works of authorship,' including literary, dramatic, musical, artistic, and certain other intellectual works. This protection is available to both published and unpublished works."

But what does that mean to you as you buy and sell at online auctions? Simply put, it means that any copyrighted material that is not being sold by the originator or licensee of the work is most likely infringing on a legal copyright registration.

Who's licensed to sell copyrighted material? The answer depends on who the copyright owner (the originator of the work) has authorized to distribute the work. Typically that means who has been granted license to reproduce and sell the work in a "tangible medium of expression," such as a CD, a DVD, a book or magazine, a poster or lithograph, or even a dramatic work.

Are infringing items, then, being offered at online auctions? Absolutely. Can the legal copyright owners or licensees claim infringement? Absolutely. Does every infringing sale get noticed and acted upon? No. But don't let the sheer volume of items being exchanged lull you into a false sense of security (or obscurity). These days, bootleggers and frauds who make a living selling copyrighted work without license and without sharing the income with the originator are diligently being hunted. Musicians, filmmakers, writers, and the like are all working to take a bite out of infringement, and auction sites especially are working alongside them to keep trading legal to the greatest extent possible.

Your Checklist to Avoid Posting Infringing Items

So what's *unsafe* to sell? Use this list to determine whether the items you wish to auction will be deemed lawful and legitimate:

- Avoid selling unlicensed items manufactured by yourself or others that bear legally registered logos or trademarks that you don't have permission to use.

- Avoid selling counterfeits (knock-offs) made to specifically resemble a licensed item, including the use of logos, markings, or other trademarked details.

- Avoid selling promotional items that are marked "Not for resale."

- Avoid selling bundled software that is delivered with computers.

- Avoid selling live recordings (audio or video) for which you do not have express permission from the performer or license holder.

- Avoid selling items that are unreleased or "beta" versions not intended for public use or display.

AuctionWatch.com has more! _____

**Read AW's extensive buyer and seller tip Understanding Copyright, at http://
www.auctionwatch.com/awdaily/tipsandtactics/sel-copy.html**

Can You Claim Copyright of Your Auctions?

Forget the items being sold for a moment. With the exceptional work many sellers are doing at online auctions to promote their items, a new question has arisen regarding who owns the content of that work. Though most everything you'll find online is easy to copy or download, that doesn't necessarily imply you're free to do so.

Consider a seller who works diligently to craft an enticing auction description, perhaps applying well-used HTML coding and exquisite digital images that have been enhanced to better present an item for sale. Along comes another seller with the same sort of item to sell and decides it's easiest to just "lift" the hard-working seller's auction listing, images and all, to promote a different auction. Foul? Probably.

Web content is generally protected by copyright law whenever original work is presented. This includes (but is not necessarily limited to) the following:

- Original text

- Original images

- Original e-mail documents

- Original Usenet postings

- Original sound and motion image files

 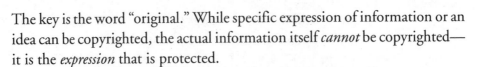
The key is the word "original." While specific expression of information or an idea can be copyrighted, the actual information itself *cannot* be copyrighted— it is the *expression* that is protected.

But at auction sites, the definition of what's copyrightable is somewhat ambiguous. In fact, it's still unclear who really can claim ownership of auction listings posted at a host site. The sites usually claim the right to post the listings but disclaim ownership or liability for the content of a listing. Sellers, on the other hand, might not be able to claim copyright of their listing if it is merely based on the restatement of generally known or recoverable facts. However, if the listing contains significant expression of information (including any original motifs, logos, or names) or other original information created by the seller, that sort of expression is probably protected by copyright law and cannot legally be "borrowed" for use by another seller without permission.

What's Wrong with a Little Infringement Between Friends?

So will you get caught selling copyrighted material when you're not the owner or aren't licensed to do so? Maybe and maybe not. Visit any of the P2P auction sites and you'll find a generous offering of such material with nary a mention of the original copyright owner or licensee. Quite often, copyright owners will turn a blind eye to this activity, realizing the amount of work it would take to track down, halt, and prosecute every violator. Again, that doesn't make it right to sell such items, but it's realistic to think you might not get into trouble.

In fact, some content owners see a little secondary market exchanging of copyrighted material as potentially good for business. Though legally this is discouraged and disallowed, the word-of-mouth potential and greater dissemination might bolster public awareness for an artist, a musician, or whomever. Provided it's not a situation that truly gets out of hand and becomes outright piracy, some content owners will consider it part of the business.

However, some content owners are adamant about protecting the rights (and potential income) of their work. In fact, many such owners are working directly with auction sites to monitor listings and to identify infringing items. If such items are found, the penalty to the infringing seller can be as simple as a *cease and desist* order (a "slap on the hand" that instructs the seller to discontinue such sales both now and forever)—but it might involve stiff fines or even imprisonment. In more blatant cases of piracy or fraud, content owners are working with federal agencies to ferret out and fully prosecute hard-core offenders.

What the Auction Sites Are Doing About Copyright Infringement

Auction sites got involved in policing their listings back in 1998, after claims of rampant fraud and illegal and infringing sales surfaced. To maintain a safe and legal trading environment and to prevent their portals from becoming absolute dens of thieves, auction sites have taken steps to clean up their act.

- Sites have posted explicit policies regarding items that are disallowed for auctioning.

- Sites provide listings of potentially questionable or infringing items as guidance for sellers.

- Sites have begun to actively monitor certain categories of items in search of illicit goods.

- Sites regularly shut down auctions of disallowed items.

- Sites regularly suspend sellers (or buyers) who are in clear violation of site policies in these matters.

- Sites have teamed up with organizations such as the National Consumer's League and the FBI to take further steps against violators.

- Sites do have certain freedom to turn over user information to official agencies when requested as part of an investigation or potential prosecution.

- Some sites, including eBay, have begun soliciting the help of the auction community to assist in identifying and reporting offending listings.

The Long Arm of the Law

So who's getting involved in bringing offenders to justice? You might be surprised to learn how visible online auctions have become in the prosecutorial community. Here's just a short list of organizations who are presently involved in scrutinizing and assisting buyers, sellers, and auction sites in matters of the goods for sale and practices in selling them:

- NCL (National Consumer's League)

- BBB Online (Better Business Bureau)

- RIAA (Recording Industry Association of America)

- MPAA (Motion Picture Association of America)

- SIIA (Software and Information Industry Association)

- FTC (Federal Trade Commission)

- INTA (International Trademark Association)

- FBI (Federal Bureau of Investigation)

Clearly, with the heightened visibility of online auctions, many national law enforcement, content owners, and consumer organizations are just as active at these sites as are bidders and sellers (though for different reasons).

AuctionWatch.com has more!

Don't miss AW's investigation of eBay's controversial Verified Rights Owner program, which is designed to remove infringing items from eBay. In "VeRO: For Better or Worse," AW explores both sides of the VeRO debate. Find it at http://www.auctionwatch.com/awdaily/features/vero/index.html

The Auction Vigilante

Then there's the man and woman on the street. Communities of involved members are what make many auction sites successful. However, some people have gone a bit overboard in deputizing themselves to strike out and rid the auction streets of "undesirables." Though their intentions are good, their methods of attack can become as undesirable as those they purport to be policing.

So even though you're minding your own business and attempting to steer clear of trouble, a Net Cop might tap you on the shoulder and inquire about your purpose for being here. Here's how you may be approached:

- You may get unexpected e-mail messages from strangers who don't seem to be potential bidders, inquiring about an auction and the item's origin.

- You may hear from an anonymous user (using a vanilla e-mail account such as HotMail) informing you of an auction site's policies or current laws that conflict with an item being auctioned.

- After you bid in an auction, you may get a message warning you about the seller and urging you to reconsider and withdraw the bid.

- After you post an auction, you may receive a threatening message warning you to halt the auction or risk being "turned in" to auction administrators and even law enforcement.

- If a host site cancels an auction, you may get a message from another user, claiming responsibility for the cancellation.

Dealing with Overzealous Net Cops

The range of activity practiced by Net Cops spans from helpful advice to unwanted harassment or threats. Take the friendly contact as just that—friendly. However, if you're uncomfortable with how some unannounced vigilante has gotten involved in your business without being authorized by an auction site or official agency, here's how you can respond:

- Ignore the contact. Remember, some are just bored or looking for an excited response. File the message away for the time being and go about your business.

- Politely respond to the sender and ask their purpose and authorization to contact you. They might be trying to help you or they might be trying to rattle you.

- Report any bothersome, harassing, or threatening messages to the hosting site immediately.

- Report any individual (or e-mail address) to proper authorities whenever you suspect someone is posing illegally as a law enforcement or agency official.

This information is not meant to cast Net Cops in an entirely dim light; there are some involved community members who are responsible and conscientious when patrolling the auction sites. In fact, most sites and other community members encourage all to become involved and not turn a blind eye or deaf ear to obvious misdeeds. Just remember to keep it within reason and turn matters over to the properly authorized individuals if a real problem arises.

 AuctionWatch.com has more!

Intrigued? Learn more about Net Cops in AW's feature story "Net Cops: To Protect and Surf?" at http://www.auctionwatch.com/awdaily/features/netcops/index.html

Know Your Rights

And what about you? Have you created something that you'd like to protect from unauthorized use, duplication, or distribution? Here's how to recognize and protect your own unique work:

- Anything you create that is an original expression in a tangible medium is immediately considered copyrighted to you whether you've officially submitted a copyright registration form or not.

- As the "author" of the work (which includes written work, paintings, photographs, music, and software), you have immediate protection for your work under the U.S. Copyright Act of 1976, which gives you exclusive rights to your work (or to others you license), whether the work is currently published or unpublished.

- Authors can grant licenses to others to exercise certain rights that would bring a work to publication, distribution, or exhibition. Any rights the author does not expressly license to another party are retained by the author (such as withholding dramatic rights or electronic rights).

In a nutshell, if it's original, if you created it, it's yours and yours alone until you give permission for someone else to reproduce or distribute it. If you are a musician and see your music being copied and sold as unauthorized CD-ROMs, your rights are being infringed. If you're a photographer and find someone restriking and selling copies of your photographs, your rights are being infringed.

Of course, to truly understand all the variations and intricacies of copyright law, it's a good idea to become familiar with U.S. Code Title 17: Copyright Law. Visit the U.S. Copyright Law Web site at http://www.loc.gov for more information. Protect your rights and protect the rights of others by understanding copyright and how it is infringed.

Key Watch Points

- As you decide the different items you intend to sell at auctions, be sure to become familiar with the site's definition of *forbidden*, *questionable*, and *infringing* items.

- Understand the importance of copyright laws and how they protect creators of original works.

- Steer clear of selling items that could be illegal or infringing, understanding that serious offenses are cause for suspension from use of an auction site, actionable by law, and could lead to fines and possible imprisonment.

- If ever in doubt, seek out help from an auction site or an official organization that can clarify if the items you want to sell will be legal and appropriate.

- When bidding, be aware of items that may be knock-offs or otherwise infringing. Not only are the items illegal, they're also usually of inferior quality.

- Be helpful to your auction community by reporting infringing or illegal auctions, but be careful not to get too carried away.

- Understand your rights as an author of an original work and be sure to notify an auction site or seek additional help if you feel your work is being reproduced or sold without your permission.

CHAPTER 10

Get Real: Authentication and Appraisal

Level:	**Intermediate to Advanced**
Reader:	**Buyer and Seller**

Can you *prove* it's real?

If so, do you know how much it's worth?

These are often the questions of the day at online auctions. Whenever you decide to buy or sell an item of perceived significance or one that is understood to be of high value, you'll need to be sure what you're buying or selling is the genuine article. With so much bad press about bogus autographs and paintings up for bid, buyers and sellers have learned it's time to either get well-schooled or seek a second (and sometimes third) opinion about the things they'll buy and sell.

And once you know something's real (or not), your next step is to use that information to determine its value. Unless it's a common item, you might need to seek special resources or other individuals to help you determine if that item is truly worth all the gold in your coffers. Appraising is all about establishing the anticipated value of authentic merchandise.

Why Authenticate?

Unless you want to buy or sell gizmos and thingamajigs that you can't properly identify and about whose value you can't be sure (meaning as a buyer you might pay too much or as a seller you might earn too little), you'll want to be confident about the items that pass through your hands. Authentication is something of a history lesson and treasure hunt, the final result often being quite revealing.

The Basic Facts

Here's what's at the core of authenticating and appraising. You can't move forward until you can answer the following questions about any item:

- *What* is the item?

- *Where* was the item made?

- *When* was the item made?

- *Who* made the item?

These questions apply to handmade items, antique items, one-of-a-kind items, and even mass-produced items. Once you've successfully answered this batch, you can move forward to the potentially exciting questions:

- *What* is it worth?

- *Who's* looking for (and paying for) one?

The Proven Benefits

Besides having a good understanding of your item and its potential value, consider these additional benefits of authentication:

- You develop a sharp eye and quick intuition for this and other related items, especially those that other buyers and sellers might overlook.

- As a seller, you determine the potential pool of customers (or collectors) who might seek such an item.

- You can provide enough facts and details about your items to instill confidence in your customers.

- You can properly position and price the auctions you hold by understanding trends and attitudes about the items you'll sell.

- You learn who your competitors in the field are, whether you're buying or selling.

- You learn the esoteric language of other enthusiasts who specialize in a certain item; speak the way the pros speak and eliminate miscommunication.

- You establish relationships with other specialists and further grow your knowledge about particular items.

- You build expertise that others will quickly recognize, possibly establishing yourself as one to consult when verification is wanted.

- You can thwart attempts by dishonest buyers or sellers who might like to dupe you in regard to the value (or purported lack thereof) of different items.

The Keys to Authentication

When authenticating, there are certain things to look for—and some general principles that can be applied to most items:

- Look for distinguishing markings such as brands, imprints, inscriptions, and so on. Many appraisers insist that this is your first duty when you identify items.

- Compare the item in question to other known genuine items. Whether in books, museums, or private collections, start with a proven authentic item and compare your item to it.

- Look for natural aging as well as attempts to "clean up" the item.

- Research the item in regard to time period created, tools and techniques available and used at the time, and linkage to other similar items.

- Consider the source: Who was this item's previous owner and how did they come to own it? What do they know about the item? Likewise, who's selling the item and what is their background or expertise in this sort of thing?

The Burden of Proof

And so, you ask, whose responsibility is it to authenticate an item?

- *The seller* is naturally most responsible for offering authentic goods whenever proclaiming them to be genuine. The seller can be accused of fraud if an item advertised as authentic ends up being anything less.

- *The buyer* is responsible for being sure of the items before bidding on them, in the spirit of *caveat emptor*. Sometimes, the buyer will be more aware of an item's origin than the seller. This is an advantage to a buyer who might have opportunity to purchase a valuable item for a very reasonable price. The buyer, of course, will be taking a risk of investing in a thought-to-be rare item that winds up being an albatross instead.

- The hosting site is responsible whenever it owns or officially represents an item for sale. The hosting site *should* take an interest in authentication even if it only serves as venue for the auctioning of goods, otherwise it risks inviting mistrust, scorn, and investigation.

Authentication is key to properly representing or recognizing items being auctioned. In most cases, it's a bit of insurance that a purchase can be made with confidence.

When Should You Authenticate?

Should you go through the steps to formally authenticate and appraise items every time you post an auction? It depends on what sorts of things you decide to sell. First, though, you need to understand the different types of authentication and appraisal services that are available to you.

Informal Appraisals

These are straightforward assessments of an item, its origin, and its perceived value per the opinion of the appraiser. When the appraiser is an expert on the type of item being appraised, informal appraisals can provide enough information to help the owner of the item understand it and what its *estimated* value might be. Informal appraisals can be made using photographs or via written or verbal description. The accuracy of the informal appraisal depends on the quality of photos or other descriptive information provided to the appraiser. Sometimes, informal appraisals can identify a significant piece—an item of significant value that deserves a more formal evaluation.

Formal Appraisals

The formal appraisal is often desirable when it looks like a real treasure is at hand or if there are many items to be appraised. In formal appraisals evaluators physically inspect an item using all manner of identification tools, such as magnifying glasses, black lights, and reference volumes. Formal appraisals, usually conducted in a person's home or at an appraiser's office, can be costly but can yield the sort of identification and written documentation that verifies the authenticity and value of an item.

What Should Be Authenticated?

This, then, raises the next question: what sorts of items deserve—even require—authentication and appraisal? Clearly, not *everything* should be subject to an appraiser's scrutiny. If you're selling some used paperbacks, the kids' toys, or the dog's old water dish, you probably needn't concern yourself with authentication. However, in the following situations you may want to authenticate:

- When dealing with high-valued items.

- When dealing with antiques, relics, and artifacts such as period furniture, art, pottery, jewelry, coins, and so on.

- When dealing with traditionally popular, high-demand, and high-value collectibles.

- When dealing with items known to be commonly counterfeited.

- When dealing with items that appear significant but that you're unable to identify with any confidence.

AuctionWatch.com has more!

Read more about the business of appraisals in AW's Approaching Appraisals tip, at http://www.auctionwatch.com/awdaily/tipsandtactics/sel-app.html

Go to the Source: Do-It-Yourself References

The good news for buyers and sellers is that the current "collector culture" we live in has resulted in a boom of reference materials and resources.

The Public Library

Hope you saved your library card. Libraries are excellent places to find older references (books, newspaper archives, periodicals) that help you trace the history of certain items and the time periods from which they emanate.

Booksellers

Again, with so much cultural interest in collectibles, antiques, and more, there has been an explosion in the number of books and magazines published (especially price guides and identification guides) that focus on even the most esoteric of items. Visit your local bookstore (or online Web store) and see how the antiques and collectibles section has grown.

Museums

Museums are no longer those stuffy institutions where housing the same old dinosaur bones and Revolutionary War spinning wheels. These days, museums cater to the interests of the public, presenting compelling exhibits—on technology, sports, and pop culture, for example—that serve as some of the best opportunities to learn little-known facts about your items. It's educational, too!

Historical Preservation and Collectors' Societies

Check for special groups, clubs, and organizations that focus on the items of your interest. Many have spawned specialized groups of collectors or historians. Find out if you can join up and be prepared to learn volumes from the experienced membership.

Web Sites

The great thing about the Web is everyone can now put up a Web site and discuss their favorite items at length. There are terrific sites, featuring pictures, sound files, and more, that are both entertaining and educational. Search for a particular item at any Web search engine portal and you'd be amazed how many "hits" come back.

Online Auctions

Of course, sometimes you don't need to look much further than the auction site at which you buy and sell. Check the listings (current and closed) to learn what others have written and shown about the items you're dealing in. Often, e-mail can open up an online friendship that helps two people share information and resources.

With the help of the resources just mentioned, you may be quite capable of identifying the items you'll buy and sell, and able to make a reasonable estimate of their value as well. Look over the different resources and compare and contrast their information. Then talk to others who share your interest in certain items for their "person on the street" insight and opinions.

Should You Use a Professional Appraiser?

Sometimes, your best efforts to authenticate and appraise simply won't be good enough. Whether you're buying unique items, selling them, or simply looking to value your own possessions, there are times you'll need to carefully consider turning to an expert for help.

To begin, understand the five most compelling situations in which independent estimations and appraisals are needed:

- For insurance purposes
- After some damaging event (fire, flood, and so on)
- After a death in the family
- After a divorce
- For debt recovery

Whether you'll be selling items or not, the preceding are situations when formal valuations are required for recovery, dissolution, or disposition of property.

Seeking a Professional Appraiser

Equally, when you're buying, selling, investing, or valuing your own property, it's sometimes prudent to seek assistance. The first step is to determine how to find an appraiser who's right for the job. Here are a few things to discuss as you begin to interact with appraisers:

- Explain what you want appraised and why (this will help you and the appraiser quickly determine whether you need a formal or informal appraisal).

- Ask how long the appraiser has been appraising.

- Identify the appraiser's specialty and whether his or her expertise will serve your identification and appraising needs.

- Determine if the appraiser is affiliated with any professional appraisal societies such as the American Society of Appraisers (ASA) or the International Society of Appraisers (ISA).

- Inquire how the appraiser will accurately identify items and how he will arrive at a value.

- Inquire about the appraiser's fees.

Service Highlight If you're in need of a simple, informal appraisal, you'll be happy to learn that AuctionWatch.com has its own online appraisal service. Staffed by long-time certified appraisal experts, AuctionWatch invites you to provide images and description of your items for review. The AuctionWatch appraisers can quickly help you better identify and understand your items. For more information, go to the AuctionWatch Appraisal and Gallery area on the AuctionWatch.com Web site.

Documenting Value and Authenticity

Whenever you arrange for an appraisal or purchase an authenticated item, you should insist on receiving legitimate documentation that notes and proves the genuineness of the item. Proper appraisal documentation should include the following:

- The appraiser's name, address, and professional title (distinction)

- The client's name and present address

- The purpose for the appraisal (for example, for insurance purposes or for liquidation)

- The complete listing of items being appraised with full written details regarding item dimensions, weight (when appropriate), age, condition, and any other distinguishing characteristics

- The appraised value of each item

- A "statement of disinterest," which indicates that the appraiser and client have no collaborative interest in the appraised value of any item appraised

- Appropriate presentation, typewritten, signed and dated by the appraiser

If you're seeking a formal appraisal, you should be sure you'll receive proper documentation of an item. Before agreeing to an appraisal, it's wise to request a sample appraisal from the appraiser to be sure your needs will be met.

If you're purchasing an item that is said to be authentic by way of professional appraisal, request a look at the appraisal documentation and be sure you can contact the appraiser if necessary to confirm the item, the appraisal, and the estimated value. Photocopies and handwritten appraisals are rarely worth the paper they're printed on and should serve as a warning flag to you.

What to Do If It's Bogus

Hopefully you won't find yourself in this unenviable situation, but often it happens: the item you own or have recently purchased winds up being a fake, a phony, a fraud. Though you've heard it several times already, remember it's a *caveat emptor* world out there, and you can be out in the cold when an item turns up less than genuine. However, here are a few avenues of recourse worth traveling.

Return the Item

Whether you bought the item online or at a brick-and-mortar establishment, you should always attempt to contact the seller and explain your discovery about the item's dubious nature. If you're dealing with a reputable individual or establishment, you may be granted a refund if an item is identified as non-genuine. Your best insurance here, of course, is to have obtained a thorough written description of the item with a guarantee of refund if the item is ever found not to be authentic.

Report a Fraud

If you believe you were intentionally duped, report the situation to the auction site, your local authorities, or the Better Business Bureau (whichever applies in your situation). You might or might not recover the price you paid, but you'll help prevent others from being taken in.

Sell the Item

Sometimes, reproductions are mistaken for genuine articles, later to be properly identified. Though the item won't be as valuable as an original, many folks will pay for such items. Your responsibility, of course, is to fess up to the item's true nature and not attempt to represent it as an original. (That's fraud, remember?)

Keep the Item

The item might still have decorative or utilitarian value to you. Make the best of it and keep it as a physical example of what *not* to buy the next time around.

Key Watch Points

- Understand the value of authentication to you and your customers.

- Assemble a reference library (or establish easy access to one) to help you learn more about the items you'll be interested in and to develop your own level of expertise.

- Be able to determine when the potential value of your item will be best served and preserved through an expert appraisal.

- Be sure to properly screen appraisers to ensure their services and expertise will meet your needs.

- Be sure all authenticated and appraised items are accompanied by appropriate, professional, and thorough documentation.

- Don't be afraid to contact a seller and request restitution if an item you purchase turns out to be non-authentic.

CHAPTER 11

Establishing and Managing Your Inventory

Level: *Intermediate to Advanced*

Reader: *Seller*

We all have something we would like to sell at one time or another. Online auctions are terrific venues for cleaning up the house and yard and bringing home a few extra dollars. However, serious sellers are in this for the longer term and must take a more focused approach to developing and growing their auction business. Once you get into that league, *inventory* is your product and budgeting and maintaining that inventory is what keeps you (hopefully) operating in the black. And just as it is important to have a steady flow of merchandise to auction at a profit, it's equally important to control that inventory to be sure you can track it, value it, and even find it when the time is ripe to sell.

Reality Check: Know Your Margins

As you approach the tasks of acquiring, maintaining, and replenishing an inventory of merchandise, your first considerations should center around costs and profits. Ask yourself:

- What will it cost to establish an inventory of the items I want to sell?

- What will it cost to store and maintain my inventory?

- What will it cost to list or advertise my inventory?

- What prices can I expect to get for my items? (Be realistic!)

- What percentage of return must I realize to make a profit?

As most sellers quickly find out, without a proper plan for covering or surpassing outgoing expenses with incoming cash, an online auction endeavor can quickly dry up before it's had a chance to flourish.

When you begin to establish your inventory plan, keep these questions in mind:

- Am I in this for the long haul or just a one-time stint?

- How much inventory do I already have, what return might it bring, and how long will it sustain my selling activity?

- How much capital (expendable cash or access to it) will I need to establish my inventory of goods?

- What sorts of goods do I want to sell? Should I generalize or specialize?

- At what prices can I purchase goods and what profit percentage can I expect to pull down?

- How popular are the items I want to sell and what kind of inventory turnover can I reasonably expect?

- How and where will I store my inventory, and does it require special environmental conditions (temperature, humidity, and so on)?

- How many auctions do I wish to stage each week or month and what levels of inventory will I need to support that?

- What is the lead time to replenish my inventory?

• Will the items I sell be seasonal—selling best at certain times of the year—or can I look for sustained sales levels year round?

As you can see, much of this revolves around the supply of your items, the demand for them, and the costs involved in acquiring, maintaining, and selling them. Though Chapter 12 will delve deeper into the details of cost versus sales, consider these aspects of inventory acquisition and management before you head off to buy up truckloads of widgets and whatchamacallits that may or may not be profitable for you.

Establishing Sources of Inventory

Most sellers have a variety of sources from which to draw items for sale. The truly prolific sellers will usually tell of finding "inventory" anywhere and everywhere (literally). Where does their great stuff come from? There are several troves that sellers are tapping on a regular basis.

Garage Sales

When you're looking to pay only pennies on the dollar, look no further than the neighbor's driveway. Garage sales are perfect for finding great items, odd items, and lightly used items that resell online at terrific profit. To truly maximize your effort when cruising the garage sales, plot a course to hit as many sales as possible within an area—and be prepared to offer a price for an entire boxload or table full of items. (Bulk offers work best near the end of the day when the seller is anxious to close down—so think about going back to sales that seem likely to have auctionable items left over.)

Flea Markets and Swap Meets

These are the garage on the grander scale, where the sellers come to you—sort of. Many sellers tell of finding great items (along with great gobs of garbage) at flea markets. The key is to arrive early. You'll be in the company of many other "pickers" and "treasure finders" who swoop down upon the various sellers looking to grab the best stuff before the sun comes up and the masses come out. Again, don't be bashful about haggling, especially if you've gone back for more shopping near the end of the day.

Thrift Stores

Sometimes, folks don't have the time or patience to attempt a sale of their own and will settle for packing up their unwanted goods and carting them off to the local thrift store. They get a receipt to take a deduction at tax time and you have a new venue to find great bargain items that folks might be paying well for at the online auctions. Warning: thrift stores are often somewhat cluttered and disorganized. Be prepared to do some serious digging.

Tag Sales and Estate Sales

These are indoor events where a private individual is selling off possessions or has hired a professional to manage the sale of items owned by someone recently deceased. Regardless, the quality of items is often a step up from what you'll find at garage sales and flea markets. Competition is a bit stiffer here and incredible bargains are more difficult to come by. However, there's still good opportunity to find deals and make purchases that you can later resell to discerning buyers for a reasonable profit.

Auctions

Of course, there's the auction in its many forms and appearances. In the physical world, be sure to visit private auctions (possibly part of an estate or tag sale), phone auctions (often geared toward collectors), and public auctions (such as those held at flea markets as well as government and police auctions). Online, many sellers tell of purchasing items for resale at the very auctions where they list their wares. It's not uncommon to find a seller offering merchandise acquired right there at a great price just a few weeks earlier. With a bit of repositioning and attention to timing, many sellers turn quite a good profit from online auction purchases.

Specialty Shows and Exhibits

Collectors and dealers regularly congregate at special shows that cater to their interests. Often, you can find interesting items at these shows that could bring a profit upon resale, but remember the dealers at the shows are there for the same purpose: to make a profit. Don't expect to find garage sale or flea market prices, but keep a keen eye open for unique items that, based on your knowledge of the online market, look underpriced at the dealer's table. And don't forget to ask what else the dealer might have that isn't currently displayed; that bargain might still be packed in a box behind the table.

Closeouts, Outlet Stores, and Wholesalers

If you decide to sell recently manufactured items, always look for the no-frills venue where you can buy a manufacturer's overstock, either from a clearance-type store or direct from the manufacturer's distributor (you'll typically require a valid resale license to purchase direct from the distributor). Be wary of loading up and relying too much on this type of merchandise to carry the bulk of your sales business, however. Though some folks have been successful reselling such items online, remember there was a reason that the merchandise was being closed out in the first place: people weren't buying it.

Networking

As it's often said, "It doesn't matter what you know; it's *who* you know." Many sellers find terrific buys and resale opportunities as a result of their interactions and relationships with others. As you make your rounds looking for new veins of inventory, get to know the people you'll rub elbows with. When people help people, the result can be most satisfying—and profitable.

AuctionWatch.com has more!

Learn more techniques in AW's extensive seller tip Building an Inventory, at http://www.auctionwatch.com/awdaily/tipsandtactics/sel-buildinginventory.html

The Goods Might Be Right Under Your Nose

If you're like most people these days, you're probably sitting on a ready-to-go inventory within your own living space. It takes practically no time at all to accumulate mounds of stuff that gets in your way, but which may be excellent auction fodder. Before you throw a pile of stuff away or donate it to a charity, look for the sorts of items listed here. They're all excellent sellers—and common items you find around the house every day.

Antiques

Do you have stuff—furniture, artwork, tools, simple appliances, statuary, and so on—that's been passed down from generation to generation? Many folks have quite a collection of odds and ends that have surpassed the 100-year mark and thereby earned the rightful name of "antique." This is the stuff that bidders are actively seeking online right now, so—provided it's not a beloved family heirloom—why not cash in?

Advertising, Premium, and Promotional Items

Remember all that mail-away stuff you and your kids clipped box tops to get? How 'bout those silly trinkets from cereal boxes that you've had stashed in your Cap'n Crunch treasure box since you were a kid? Gas station giveaways? Fast food toys? Take a close look around and see if you have any of this stuff that has aged 20 years or more. Chances are, there's a good market for it online.

China and Silverware

You may be sitting on a gold mine disguised as a buffet or china cabinet. Check it closely—that awful stuff that sits there year after year because you don't want to look at it could be quite valuable.

Old Product Packaging

It's not just Prince Albert in a can that draws the attention of collectors. Today, folks are bidding handsomely for product paraphernalia such as old cans, spice tins, soda bottles, cereal boxes, and just about anything else that conjures up memories of years past.

Anything in the Kids' Room

If your kids are at least into their 30's today, you can expect that anything that may have remained in your attic from their youth is commanding good prices online. Toys, games, comics, trading cards, posters, records (and 8-track tapes), and other relics from the 1970s and earlier have become quite desirable to others in their age bracket. Of course, your kids know this too and will probably be visiting any day now to reclaim their treasures.

Practically everything and anything is auctionable these days. If you've been meaning to get around to decluttering your living spaces, take a second look and determine if what you have lurking in the garage, attic, back bedroom, or even at the off-site storage facility is the kind of thing folks online would love to pay you for. Most often, that stuff is inventory and you should retrieve, catalog, and list it as such.

Reinvestment: Budget and Buy for Resale

You already understand that one great buy or an attic full of stuff isn't going to be enough to support your auction business for an extended period. Though you can do well in online sales while your great stuff lasts, when your intention is to sell for the long haul you're going to need to develop a profit-friendly method of replenishing your stocks. That means buying with an eye on resale goals. Therefore, be sure to consider the following *before* you make your inventory investments:

- Can you purchase an item or items at a price that affords you reasonable profit?

- How quickly can you resell your prospective purchase? You don't want your money tied up in inventory for too long.

- Is there demand for the item that has been proven in the online auction arena?

- If you're dealing in collectibles, do you know which items are more elusive and which are more common? You'll want to hunt down the elusive items to make larger profits. (Hint: Talk with other sellers and dealers to learn what their customers are most eager to purchase, then explore the availability of those items for yourself.)

- Is there an upcoming event (news development, movie release, and so on) that could repopularize a particular item or group of items you have a chance to purchase cheaply?

Your key to sound inventory investment is to either have a good mix of items that appeals to many customers or a focused set of items that are sought after by serious buyers. Whichever route you take, be sure that you can gain a return on your investment by at least 75 to 150 percent (and higher is always better), including allowances for business expenditures—which you'll read more about in Chapter 12.

Tools and Techniques to Keep Track of It All

So here you are with your terrific, cost-effective, and profit-bearing inventory of great items. But what a mess! How will you ever get it all in order, easily identifiable, and properly documented in a way that will streamline your efforts while helping you track the health of your business? Organization of your inventory will be a key asset to you and will make your business run more cost-effectively. First, you'll need a system to maintain data related to your inventoried items.

AW Auction Manager Pro

AuctionWatch.com's downloadable bulk loader also acts as an inventory management system, in which sellers can import and save relevant sales data related to their items. Instead of arduously inputting inventory data, such as each item's title, description, price, Quantity, SKU, and more, into a spreadsheet program, create an "Inventory Item" within Auction Manager Pro.

From AM Pro, sellers then can bulk upload hundreds of items at once, including appropriate data stored in your "Inventory Items." Auction Manager Pro also features support for AW image hosting, counters, and templates.

AW Inventory Management

This is great online tool for high-volume sellers and businesses that sell similar items on a regular basis. Enter your item once, and it's ready to launch on multiple auction sites over and over again, whenever you please. The AW Inventory Management system allows you to create and organize thousands of items.

Now, consider the information you'll want to enter into Auction Manager Pro's Inventory Item form:

- **Title**. What is it?

- **Description**. Detailed description that highlights unique attributes of the item.

- **Additional Comments/Notes**. Record special data, such as the item's estimated value, purchase date, purchase location, and storage area.

- **Images**. Attach an existing image in AM Pro to your auction or upload a new image to AM Pro for an auction. Even preview images within AM Pro.

- **Avg. Item Cost**. How much did you pay for it? (Don't forget to keep all your receipts.)

- **Original Qty**. How many did you start with?

- **Qty Sold**. How many have you sold?

- **Qty in Stock**. How many do you have left in stock?

- **Starting Bid**. Enter a default starting bid for an item

- **Reserve**. Enter a default reserve price for an item

- **Instant Buy**. Enter a default take-it-price for an item

- **UPC/ISBN**. Universal Product Code, International Standard Book Number; record the item manufacturer's product codes.

Storage Concerns

Many sellers can tell tales of woe about the time when they didn't have a good storage system. Whether an item got lost or damaged, inadequate attention to storage has cost them in the long run. Though you might begin with a small table full of items to sell, be aware that your inventory can quickly swell to fill up desk drawers, closet spaces, and whole rooms. So, what should you consider as you decide where you'll store your inventory?

- How big (or small) will the items be? If you're selling furniture or other large items, you'll be faced with the need for a larger storage area than if you're selling knickknacks.

- Does the inventory require climate control? All items are best stored in clean, dry environments, but some items need special care in regard to humidity and exposure to sunlight.

- Can the inventory be secured? Though you may trust your friends and family, you will want to be able to "close up" your inventory area to ensure nothing is inadvertently moved or misplaced. And, of course, truly valuable items such as jewelry and the like should be locked up for safety's sake.

- How large will the inventory grow? Though you may start off with low expectations, many sellers who find their rhythm tell of storage facilities that were quickly outgrown. Keep expansion in mind and be prepared to deal with overflow from your initial storage solution.

- Will storage cost? Some sellers have so much inventory that they have to move much of it to off-site storage facilities. Keep those costs in mind as you figure the rest of your selling expenses and profit expectations.

- How accessible will the inventory be? If your items are stored off-site or up in the attic, always work to keep items relatively within reach. Clambering over boxes or trying to access an off-site facility with limited business hours could become inconvenient and time-consuming.

Rotate Your Stock, Follow the Trends

Remember that Pokemon won't be hot forever nor will there be consistent demand for beach balls or fast-aging PC goods. Give your inventory a "shelf life" and try to keep it moving in line with public demand. You'll want to avoid some common traps that lie in wait for sellers.

If It's Hot Today It's Gotta Be Hot Tomorrow

Wrong—it's much better to figure it will be cold tomorrow. Trends and fads are commonplace—think of Cabbage Patch dolls, Furbies, and Y2K paraphernalia. Buy before or just at the onset of the newest craze and sell as it peaks. Your goal is to have your inventory depleted before everyone else catches on and floods the market with similar goods.

It's Bound to Be Popular One of These Days

Avoid investing heavily on trendy merchandise that could take years to ever "mature" (that is, to develop a significant rise in value long after the demise of the original burst of popularity). Some items can be an instant gold mine while others simply languish. To you, that's either cash that's forever tied up or a loss if you decide to dump the goods for whatever they'll bring.

Nobody Shares the Really Good Information

Actually, trade papers and collector's reports are full of useful news about buyers' changing attitudes. Never before have buyers been so bombarded with appeals for their money and you'll need to read widely to be at precisely the right place with the right stuff at the right time.

The Older It Gets, the More It'll Be Worth

Avoid holding inventory too long in anticipation of potentially higher profits. Find your profit goal and, if the market will meet it, sell. If you wait too long to sell, hoping for even higher profits, demand might fall off quickly and you might find that the opportunity has ended as quickly as it first appeared.

Key Watch Points

- Determine your sales goals before you begin investing in inventory.

- Identify the sorts of items you wish to sell and determine which venues will serve as the best sources for replenishing your inventory.

- Don't forget to look around you: your present belongings can be one of the best immediate sources of items to sell.

- As you build and replenish your inventory, be careful to consider resale potential as well as storage needs.

- Roll with the trends: keep your inventory fresh and in demand to help ensure your cash assets don't get tied up for extended periods of time.

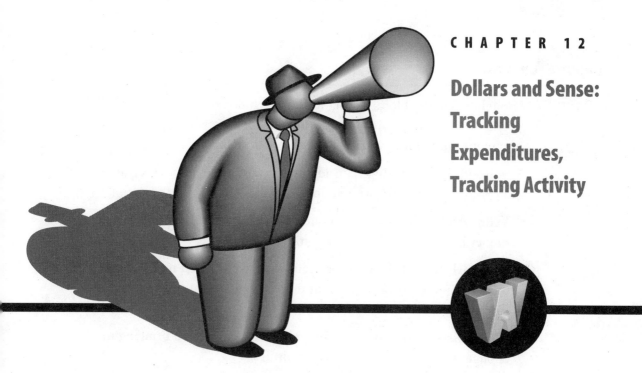

CHAPTER 12

Dollars and Sense: Tracking Expenditures, Tracking Activity

Level: *Intermediate to Advanced*

Reader: *Seller*

The bids are coming in, the inventory is shipping out, and you feel that you're an unquestionable success. At the end of the day, however, will you be able to put your finger on precisely what you've spent, how much you've made, and what it all means to your bottom line? To be really sure your business is going in the right direction, you'll need to make sure you're keeping costs under control, records up to date, and tomorrow's goals within reach. Put on your accountant's visor because this is where you'll see how good your business looks on paper.

Balance Your Budget

Though members of local and national governments struggle with it at every go-round, balancing your budget is not such a harrowing tightrope walk as you might think. However, it does require effort and diligence.

As you approach budgeting, consider that you'll be looking to keep an eye on and control over the following points:

- **Your cash flow**. How much money are you spending and how much money are you earning month to month?

- **Your cash cycle**. When do you regularly need to invest money in your business and when can you count on receiving income as a return on that investment?

- **The realistic nature of your financial success**. Are you bringing in enough income to cover your expenditures?

- **The flexibility of your budget**. Does it respond to spikes and dips in your business, possibly in line with seasonal factors that might affect your business?

- **The bottom line**. How much money are you really making, how much can you safely consider *wages,* that is, the profit from your business that pays you for your efforts?

The Numbers Rarely Lie

And, as developing a budget can be an intimidating prospect, keep in mind that taking an analytical view of your cash flow will help you determine how you should establish your business, how well you might expect to do, and what you think it will cost to reach your goal. In your planning, be sure to think about the following:

- Will this be a part-time or a full-time venture? The answer will dictate how aggressive your financial goals need to be.

- Will what you intend to sell be more cost-laden than some other sort of commodity? Consider initial cost of inventory, special storage needs, shipping costs, and so on.

- As you budget for inventory, consider how much time you'll have each month to turn your goods around and help ensure inventory doesn't accumulate too much faster than you can sell it.

So, in a nutshell, make sure your budget accounts for the following:

- Your starting balance of cash and assets.

- Your anticipated costs during the month (or whatever accounting period you decide to adopt).

- A buffer or safety net of funds for unexpected costs.

- Your desired profit (positive incoming cash flow) after all costs have been deducted.

Once you've developed what you consider a working budget, keep a close eye on it and monitor your actual activity as compared to your budgeted activity as often as week to week, or even day to day. At the end of the month, determine how closely your actual activity matched your anticipated (budgeted) activity. Tweak your figures and revisit your bottom line to be sure your business is staying on a growing and profitable track.

AuctionWatch.com has more!

For more on this topic, read AW's Bidding on a Budget tip, at http://www. auctionwatch.com/awdaily/tipsandtactics/buy-budget.html

Balance Your Inventory

In Chapter 11 you read about how you might assemble your inventory to support your auctions. Here, consider the deeper financial ramifications of the style of inventory you keep and how that can affect your operating budget. It's not rocket science here, but don't overlook a few key points that can have significant impact on how your business runs and how your cash flows.

- Will your inventory consist of high-end goods that, even at reseller costs, involve significant expense?

- Will your inventory require additional insurance and other protection that you'll need to add to your list of regular expenditures?

- Can your inventory be easily replaced if damaged, lost, or stolen?

- Can you be relatively sure of making regular sales throughout the year (or whatever your targeted selling season will be)?

- If selling extremely low-end goods, can you sell enough items to bring in significant levels of income?

- Can you modify your inventory easily throughout the year to ensure that some kinds of merchandise can pick up the slack when sales of other merchandise trail off?

Inventory balance is important to ensure that you can always have sales coming in and you can always replenish with something you know will contribute to your bottom line. The good news is that you can tailor your inventory to suit your goals whether you want to sell high-end goods, low-end goods, seasonal goods, or year-round favorites.

Service Highlight

Just when you needed it most, AuctionWatch.com offers a new Inventory Management tool. Use it to catalog your inventory, keep a running record of its value, catalog images, and more. You'll find it in the Auction Manager section of AuctionWatch.com.

Balance Your Time

Any time you spend on one part of your business is time you give up on another. One key to understanding the value of your time is to understand what efforts tend to bring the biggest dividends. If you're a one-person show (as many on the auction circuit are), you'll need to spread your time-wealth wisely and judiciously to ensure no part of your business suffers.

To that end, consider the amount of time you spend on different activities and how you might improve your efficiency.

Replenishing Your Inventory

Do you spend a lot of time on the road, visiting various places to find exciting new things to sell? Are the finds worth your time? If you think you're spending too much time finding goods to sell, consider these options:

- See if you can acquire merchandise by using the telephone or by ordering online.

- Determine which sources seem to provide the best merchandise—the stuff that sells most often and at the best profits—and focus your time on those sources.

- Designate certain days of the week when you'll hit the road to find goods and work to a plan (plot out a course or choose certain source points that are within the same geographic area).

- Enlist the help of other dealers, friends, and family members to notify you when they encounter the items you like to sell.

Listing Items

This can sometimes take more time than you realize. If you're making fancy listings, does the extra effort payoff or are you spending too much time on auctions that will only pull down a few bids and a few dollars? If you're busily listing everything under the sun, do all your listings result in sales? Consider these tactics to make your listing more time- and cost-effective:

- Invest your time in sprucing up the auctions that will have the most promise for a good sale. Don't waste frosting on day-old bread.

- Enlist the use of a bulk lister whenever possible to make listing as simple as a mouse-click or two.

- Designate a day (or days) of the week when you'll list.

- Consider using Dutch auctions if you want to move more than one identical item with a single listing.

- Pay attention to the items that seem to sell well and consider dropping those that fail to get bids.

Packing and Shipping Items

This can also take considerable time, depending on how many items you sell each month and how organized your shipping routine is. If you're forever up to your elbows in shipping tape and packing peanuts, consider a different approach:

- Time your auctions so you'll be able to better control when you'll need to pack and ship items.

- Prepack items and keep them in a holding area until the winning bidder's payment arrives.

- Make use of free postage supplies and preprinted labels whenever possible.

- Without delaying your shipments, try to make your trips to the post office or carrier office count by shipping many items at once.

- Investigate using online postage services (eStamp.com or Stamps.com) to have your packages preposted, avoiding waiting in line to have your items metered.

- Investigate carrier home pickup services.

Handling Administrivia

Sending end-of-auction notifications and responding to all sorts of e-mail can get time consuming. It's important to do, but it can easily be overdone to the point that you spend more time than you should e-chatting and less time tending to other areas of your business.

- Keep up on your e-mail by responding the moment you receive a message.

- Keep your records up to date daily or designate a day to do your book work.

- Use software applications that auto-generate e-mail messages and others that help you automate your record keeping.

Researching Your Market

Keep abreast of latest developments not only in the online auction world but also in your field of expertise. At the same time, don't fall into analysis paralysis to the point that you feel compelled to spend hours of research time before feeling confident about listing your next item or expanding into a new sort of merchandising. The pertinent facts can usually be found floating near the top.

Taking a Break

Just as you can't expect to keep your nose to the grindstone endlessly, you also can't rest on your laurels too long either. All business owners deserve a well-earned respite to remind themselves the reason for their toil. However, too much lounging about can be habit-forming and suddenly, the time off equates to a drop-off in income.

AuctionWatch.com has more!

For more on this topic, read AW's Timesaving Strategies tip, at http://www.auctionwatch.com/awdaily/tipsandtactics/sel-timesave.html

Record Your Expenses

Though part of the appeal of online auctioning is its relatively low cost, many hard-core sellers get a real eye opener when they sit down and tally their per-auction costs. And many others overlook the other expenses associated with buying and selling online. The only way to be sure you can confidently determine if your business is profitable is to recognize and record each of these expenses:

- **Internet fees**. Unless you're using one of those "free Internet" services, you're probably paying a monthly fee for Internet access. That's a cost of doing business, so record it.

- **Storage and insurance fees**. If you've moved your inventory off-site or are paying insurance to protect its value, that's another expense to consider.

- **Listing fees**. Most sites charge a small fee to list an item for auction. Though the fee rarely exceeds $2, listing a hundred items or more can add up pretty quickly.

- **Special feature fees**. If you want special fonts, icons, category placement, or price protection, understand the fees that are associated (and some can take quite a bite out of your income—be certain the payoff has a chance to cover the cost before you indulge).

- **Sales commissions (final value fees)**. When your auction ends, the site will usually levy a commission that is a percentage of the final high bid price.

- **Shipping and handling**. The buyer is typically responsible for these costs, so you're OK for outgoing goods. When you're buying for resale, don't forget to capture these costs and add them to your cost of goods sold.

- **Insurance and tracking**. A subset of shipping and handling, but one that isn't always recorded on the postal meter.

- **Money transfer fees**. If you're using an online payment service, an escrow service, or simply purchasing money orders, don't forget the cost of using these payment methods.

- **Travel**. Whether you're off hunting for more inventory or simply driving to the carrier's office to drop off packages, there's a cost involved in whatever method you use to make the trek—be it plane, train, or automobile.

- **Supplies**. Shipping supplies, office supplies, and anything else you need to buy to make your auction business work is an expense that you need to recognize.

Document the Details

You might discover additional expenses that you incur as a part of doing business. Whatever those business expenses are, be sure you identify them and document them properly. Generally, here's the information you should make note of for every business expense:

- When the expense occurred

- Where the expense occurred

- The amount of the expense

- The business applicability of the expense

Be sure to see Chapter 15 for more details about business expenses you can legally write off come tax time.

AuctionWatch.com has more! _____

For more on this topic, read AW's Keeping Records tip, at http://www. auctionwatch.com/awdaily/tipsandtactics/sel-records.html

Record Your Sales

If you've done a good job of cataloging your inventory, recording sales is merely an extension of your item records. Refer back to the section of this chapter that discussed the information you'll want to document for your inventory. Then, when you make a sale, be sure to capture this additional information:

- Date of sale

- Sale price

- Customer

- Gain or loss (based on your original purchase price)

- Date payment received

- Payment method

- Payment processing fee (as with credit cards)

- Shipping date

- Shipping expenses

You'll notice that some of the aforementioned information will be necessary for your annual tax records while other bits will be suitable for developing a customer record and an audit trail for the completion of the transaction. All of this information is either necessary or highly useful to keep your business under control and help you quickly extrapolate important income information as well as resolve any problems that occur during the transaction.

Watch Your Assets

Back in Chapter 5, I talked about getting organized and setting up an auction office. But establishing a nice office with all sorts of great tools to help you in your work is only the beginning. Part of keeping control of your auction expenses will also include keeping an eye on how your tools are holding up. Do they require maintenance? Will they be due for replacement? Whether your printer needs a new ink cartridge or your PC monitor fizzles out, be sure to keep track of the often-overlooked costs of keeping your office machinery and other equipment up and running.

Prepare for Hard Times

Then there's the reality check that goes something like this: what if your auction business takes a nosedive? How will you survive lean times? Well, there's not really a checklist to this discussion. The simple truth of the matter is that you need to be prepared for tight times—the online auction market can change as quickly and unpredictably as the wind.

Any business counselor will advise that all entrepreneurs maintain a safety of at least six months' worth of living expenses. This will be especially true if your sales might be considered seasonal. For that matter, many auction sites have seen a seasonal slump in activity that usually occurs during the summer months when a lot of potential sellers and bidders are on vacation.

Though you may be thoroughly excited about some great initial sales of items, keep yourself grounded and recognize that not all auctions are high-flying successes. Make sure you have a little nest egg to draw on when the excitement dies down a bit.

Key Watch Points

- Understand that any business venture needs to be firmly supported by a financial plan and recognition of the costs of doing business.

- Develop a clear goal for your auction business and determine what sorts of resources will be required to meet that goal.

- Develop a budget to help you predict and control your startup as well as ongoing business costs.

- Review your budget regularly to check that you're keeping your business above water.

- Be rigorous in recording all or your business: from inventory to expenses to sales, keep all pertinent data that will help you better report, analyze, and monitor your business activity.

- Don't fall into the trap of thinking your business will be roses at every turn; there are bumps in the road and you'll need to be properly prepared to endure some less-than-stellar times.

PART III

The Evolution
of Your
Business

Level:	Advanced
Reader:	Seller

So you're ready for the big time, are you? Good. Many sellers have found a level of ongoing success that soon has them itching to take the next step beyond routine listing and selling of merchandise to establishing and advancing an actual business portal of their own. Thanks to the Internet, practically anyone can set up a viable business entity provided they have a product to sell and a motivation to succeed. For many folks, online auctions are equivalent to dipping a toe in the water to see if buying, selling, and interacting with others is really their cup of tea.

If you've been following along up to this point and have found enough success to whet your appetite, then it's time to stop testing the waters and consider jumping in with both feet.

A Self-Assessment to Determine If You're Ready to Become a Merchant

It's really quite straightforward: take a look at the following statements, make an honest assessment, and see if you're ready to step up your business potential.

You know you're ready to move ahead when:

- You find the auction venues are more limiting than enhancing to your overall business potential.

- You find you have established a customer base—that is, you have a rapport with many different individuals who are eager to know what merchandise you'll offer next.

- You've established a routine with your auction sales that allows you to work a reasonable amount of hours while pulling down a decent and consistent income for the effort expended.

- You have seen other opportunities to serve your customers that go beyond what can and is being done at the auction venues.

- You're eager to learn and apply new skills, be they computer oriented, sales oriented, or research oriented.

- You're financially able to extend yourself into additional sales venues that may require additional commitment of time and money.

- You've already begun to draw a consistent income from activity outside the auction venues and are ready to shift more effort to it.

Then again, you may wish to give it more thought if:

- You enjoy auctioning but are rather sporadic with your listing efforts.

- You are easily distracted by temptations to surf off and shop instead of focusing on selling.

- You dread having to box up stuff to ship it out.

- You avoid competition.

- You aren't quite comfortable with online business and interactions with strangers.

- You can't afford to invest any more time in online sales.

- You're generally too reserved to ever consider promoting yourself.

If you're considering taking the leap and becoming a merchant, you need to be able to honestly assess your skills, desires, drive, and aptitudes. Many folks play at the online auctions, bringing in some extra cash here and there. That's one kind of success. Others, though, are driven to build the better mousetrap and are eager to give the public what it really wants, earning cash in the process. That's another kind of success. It's all a matter of deciding what success means to you, and how hard you're willing to work to grab the brass ring. It's not necessarily easy to break into the merchant ranks, but bear in mind that more and more regular folks are doing it—successfully—every day.

Your Reputation Precedes You

Word of mouth is alive and well online. In fact, it's that same word of mouth that routinely makes or breaks serious auction sellers. In the auction world, you know it as *feedback systems*—the public boards where buyers and sellers post comments about one another and hopefully build an online reputation to be proud of.

In the typically faceless online world, you might wonder why a reputation would be so important. Here are a few reasons:

- Most people are hesitant about engaging in business with others online: it's often a sight-unseen, I-don't-know-you, you-don't-know-me relationship.

- Most sellers doing business online aren't backed by a full-fledged business structure such as a major company.

- People are unsure what guarantees or recourse they'll have in case a problem with a transaction ever arises.

- People are afraid of being ripped off in online transactions, largely thanks to the significant incidence of online fraud.

One of your earliest goals in "going merchant" is to establish yourself as a viable seller who is fair, honest, and trustworthy. Unfortunately, simply stating that those are your personal values won't be enough to convince your customers. You'll need to build a reputation that will speak for itself.

Build a Good Auction Feedback Rating

Since you've probably decided to become a merchant thanks to your successes at online auctions, the feedback ratings you've built at the venues are your best springboard to furthering your reputation. Therefore, be diligent in establishing a feedback rating by doing the following:

- Be a good buyer and start your feedback with positive comments from other sellers.

- Become a seller and reward your buyers with good feedback for which they will reciprocate.

- Extend extra effort for your customers in the way of prompt service, polite and professional behavior, and true commitment to customer satisfaction.

- Don't be too bashful to ask your customers to post positive feedback for you after a good transaction—people sometimes forget to post their comments and a friendly reminder is typically welcome.

 AuctionWatch.com has more! _____

Read AW's extensive buyer and seller tips, Building Feedback and Requesting Feedback, at

http://www.auctionwatch.com/awdaily/tipsandtactics/sel-build.html

and

http://www.auctionwatch.com/awdaily/tipsandtactics/buy-request.html

- Work hard to satisfy all of your customers, even the difficult ones, and develop a good method of dealing with all situations. When you can turn an enemy to a friend, you've developed a skill that customers will recognize and appreciate.

AuctionWatch.com has more! _____

See AW's extensive Dealing with Difficult Buyers tips, at http://www.auctionwatch.com/awdaily/tipsandtactics/sel-difficult.html

- Once you have built a good feedback rating, consider linking to it if and when you decide to post a business Web site. It will serve as an early reference for your new customers who visit your site.

Provide Information about Yourself and Your Business

Often, customers want to know more about you or your business in order to feel more comfortable in dealing with you. Therefore, develop one of those "About Me" pages hosted by auction venues and tell people more about yourself.

- List your products and services.
- Provide a customer satisfaction statement.
- Provide a business goal statement.
- List your business methods such as fees, business hours, and so on.
- List your hobbies.
- Provide a picture of yourself (folks often feel better once they've *seen* who they're dealing with).
- Have fun and show some humor.

AuctionWatch.com has more! _____

Learn more about creating an About Me page in AW's Tips & Tactics section, at http://www.auctionwatch.com/awdaily/tipsandtactics/sel-aboutme.html

Be a Source of Help and Information

If you don't have what a customer is looking for, perhaps you know who does. If you don't have the facts regarding what a customer is asking, perhaps you know where to find them. Customers are typically impressed when a seller exhibits a level of concern for their needs beyond what that seller can provide directly. Though you may not get a particular sale when you steer customers elsewhere, you will gain their trust that you're truly interested in what they want, and that speaks volumes for your reputation.

Post Additional Customer Testimonials

With their permission, consider posting customer comments on a Web site, especially those who have done business directly at your site. Testimonials are sought after by others looking for confidence in online dealings (which is why auction feedback systems are so popular).

Get—and Stay—Organized

Though your customers probably won't ever see your physical place of business, they'll be able to tell if you're working to a plan simply by how quickly and efficiently you can respond to them. Whether they've purchased something from you or are just seeking information, your commitment to being organized will help you meet their needs and help them see that you're on top of your business.

The Do-It-Yourself Marketing Campaign

You have a terrific business plan and you've got the goods people want. Now you just need to get noticed. These days you have an opportunity to promote yourself and your business like never before. Forget sandwich boards and handbills; here's how you can hawk your wares without looking like a fly-by-night operation.

Decide Whether to Create a Web Site

Most online entrepreneurs now know that Web sites are among the easiest and most effective ways to get noticed. However, not all Web sites are created equal and not all sites will effectively achieve their goals (or yours!). As you consider your business Web site, first consider the following:

- What products or services will you sell?

- Who will your customers be and what are their needs, likes, and desires?

- How often will you need to update your site?

- How will your site promote and tie back to your other selling activities (such as your auction sales)?

- Who is your competition? Don't get overwhelmed by this, but be aware of who might be trying to carve a similar niche and what steps they've taken to do so.

- What other similar sites have you seen? What did you like about them and what didn't you like?

Build Your Web Site

As you embark on actually assembling your site, keep these thoughts in mind.

- Keep it simple and easy to navigate.

- Be sure it will load quickly—visitors won't hang around long if it takes minutes for your pages to load.

- Be sure it works! Test, test, test.

- Be sure it's running on a stable server. (Watch out for free servers—they have a tendency to go down frequently, so if you use one, keep checking to see what your customers will find.)

- Provide plenty of useful links but keep annoying advertising and bannering to a minimum.

- Provide easy contact links for your visitors to use to communicate with you.

- Establish your sales policies and ordering methods clearly.

- Get to the point: show the visitors the goods and not your skills at Web authoring.

- Keep it fresh by listing new merchandise to sell, removing sold merchandise, and listing new information or links that might be useful to your visitors.

AuctionWatch.com has more! _____

Dress up your listings or your Web site—read AW's extensive seller tip, Learning HTML, at http://www.auctionwatch.com/awdaily/tipsandtactics/sel-html.html

Promote Your Web Site

Once you have a well-designed and well-functioning site, you'll want to let the world know you're open for business. Here are some of the easiest and most effective ways to do just that.

- Register your site with search engines. There's a whole gang of search sites out there on the Web, so begin by registering your site with some of the biggest engines first (such as Yahoo, Lycos, and Alta Vista). Be sure to include all appropriate metadata to tell the indexers what can be found on your site; doing so will help your site show up on more searches.

- Link your site to your auctions. If you'll still be running auctions at the online venues (and why shouldn't you?), add a link in your item description that takes bidders to your page.

- Link your site to other sites. When you find other sites that complement yours, check with the Webmasters to see if they'll add a link to your site. Be sure to return the favor and you'll be networking with others on the Web in no time.

- Develop a mailing list. Provide a link on your site that allows visitors to be included in a regular mailing list and product update. Since it's an "opt-in," you needn't worry about being accused of spamming. Plus, many recipients will probably share the message with their friends, who soon might be telling their friends, and so on, and so on, and so on. . . .

- Become a member of an online consumer advocacy organization. Nothing speaks louder about your commitment to good business than when visitors see logos from BBBOnline (the Better Business Bureau) or other such groups. Once you're a member, organizations will allow you to display their logo on your site.

AuctionWatch.com has more!

Concerned about Privacy issues? Read AW's feature, "Getting Personal: Privacy and Online Auctions" at http://www.auctionwatch.com/awdaily/features/privacy/index.html

Maintain Your Web Site

No one likes a stale site, least of all your customers. One of the biggest challenges to new online merchants is keeping their site current. What should you keep fresh on your pages?

- Your inventory, of course.

- News about your products (new releases, industry developments, and so on).

- Special stories that relate to your products or that your customers will relate to.

- News about upcoming merchandise, sales, contests, giveaways, or any other promotional efforts you'll undertake.

- Your links. Many useful sites change their URLs or cease to exist. Keep your links to other sites current as, hopefully, others will be keeping yours current, too.

Calling in the Experts

If the home-grown approach isn't for you, if you've seen great return on your own efforts yet still feel there is an untapped potential for your business, or if you just want some additional advice on some of the fringe areas of your business, you might consider calling in some helpers. The nice thing about this sort of Web business approach is there's a lot of help sites that won't cost you an arm, leg, or your business's first-quarter profits to boost your knowledge and increase your results.

Smalloffice.com

This site offers a plethora of free commentary, instruction, and tutorials, as well as for-purchase instruction and advice to help grow your small business. You'll find everything from Web development to market research to finances to law, all presented with the small business owner in mind. Take a look—and be prepared to stay awhile.

The Small Business Advisor

Located at http://www.isquare.com, this site, developed and maintained by Information International, focuses on assisting entrepreneurs who are just starting out or are looking to advance their businesses. There's a ton of information on this site and it's another at which you could easily spend hours combing through all the useful stuff.

Bizoffice.com

Another site that offers all sorts of tools, information, and advice to entrepreneurs. Check out the easy search engine submit tool to index your site at over 2,000 search engines and directories.

SquareTrade.com

Here's a site that offers assistance in problem resolution. It's sort of a twist on BBBOnline, but SquareTrade will also assist buyers and sellers in reaching mutual understanding and agreement, even if an impartial mediator is required to help both parties sort out the situation. SquareTrade offers a logo that you can include on your Web site (upon registration) to show your customers your interest in doing good business.

AuctionWatch.com has more!

For more on Online Mediation, see AW's feature story "Neutral Third Party: Online Mediation," at http://www.auctionwatch.com/awdaily/features/neutral/index.html

Profile Your Customers

This is a sort of "before and after" exercise as well as one you'll want to conduct regularly throughout the life of your business. Big corporations spend millions of dollars every year on customer profiling, seeking to better understand their industry, their customers, and what sells and why. For you, millions of dollars aren't required to get useful and telling information on who's visiting your site, what they're doing while they are there, and how they found you in the first place.

Service Highlight

Use AW's Customer Management tool, located within Auction Manager, to establish and manage an ongoing sales relationship with your customers. Learn how at http://www.auctionwatch.com/help/acp/crmtool-howto.html

You probably did some up-front work back when you were deciding what product or service you wanted to offer. Since keeping pace with ever-changing customer consciousness is your ongoing responsibility, here's a restatement of what initial (as well as ongoing) customer profiling should include:

- **Your target customers**. Are they male or female? Young or old? Do you know their average income? Do you know why they're buying what you're selling?

- **The size of your customer pool**. Is it growing or shrinking? Is it seasonal or year round? Do other economic events have a direct impact on customer purchasing decisions?

- **Regional considerations**. Do the bulk of your customers reside in a certain geographic region, either stateside or elsewhere in the world? If so, why and what can you do to tailor your sales to specific regional needs or desires?

AuctionWatch.com has more!

Interested in going global? Read AW's extensive seller tip, Selling Internationally, at http://www.auctionwatch.com/awdaily/tipsandtactics/sel-international.html

- **Your Competition**. Be aware of pricing, service level, and anything else the competition might be offering that will draw away your customers.

With a finger on the market pulse, look deeper into your customers' wants and desires and see if you're serving up what they're looking for in key areas:

Price

To truly understand your customers, you need to understand their perception of what your product is worth. Understand when higher prices drive customers away (they can get it cheaper elsewhere) or draw them in (they perceive increased quality when they pay slightly more). Understand what the market will bear and which items will gain you different levels of profit.

Value

Not the same as price, value involves how useful the customers will perceive what you provide to be, not only in inventory or price, but also in quality, service level, and reassurance. What "creature comforts" are your customers most wanting, and can you cater to those wants?

Availability

Simply put, are your customers willing to wait for a particular item, one you say you can get but don't have at the current moment, or do they want their goods *now?* Some customers are willing to wait for an item knowing that you're capable of providing it to them in a way that pleases them. Others might be looking for the first item they can find and don't have the luxury or inclination to delay the acquisition.

Guarantees

Many items don't really require guarantees, but many more (especially in the online collecting realm) do. But you don't always have to promise the world to help your customers feel assured in their purchases. What simple guarantees are they looking for, how can you assure them about the quality or authenticity of an item *before* the sale, and what might the cost be to your business when you honor your guarantee?

AuctionWatch.com has more! _____

Read AW's extensive seller tip on the pluses and minuses of "Offering Refunds and Guarantees" at http://www.auctionwatch.com/awdaily/tipsandtactics/sel-refunds.html

Follow-up

Some customers want to make a purchase and never be bothered again. Some want to feel that you are a valuable connection that they can call upon again and again. And some want *you* to keep *them* posted about new items, offers, or other opportunities that would interest them. Determine if your customers want to build a lasting relationship with you and your business or if they'd rather be left alone to browse at their discretion.

Assuming you've learned about your customers and their desire for your products, you need to understand how well your business is serving them. Here, though, concern yourself with how well your business presence—your Web site—is performing to make visits to your storefront a pleasant and sales-generating experience. Here are some of the things you'll need to monitor:

- Which areas of your Web site are visited most?

- What days of the week do the majority of visits occur?

- How long do visitors spend at your site (including at different areas within your site)?

- How were visitors directed to your site?

- How many visitors turn into customers?

- How effective are your advertisements (banner ads) in terms of click-through usage?

- How effective are partner sites' links to directing their visitors to your site?

- How many errors occur at your site?

Though this is a lot to keep track of, the good news is that there are Web tools that help you put all of this information and more in easy-to-retrieve and easy-to-analyze forms. A *Web traffic analyzer* is a tool that's designed to help Webmasters (and businesspersons like yourself) keep a good eye on how a site is performing. Where do you get a Web traffic analyzer? Check out these products—they're available for free introductory download.

- **WebLogManager Pro**: This product is available for a 30-day trial at http://www.monocle-solutions.com.

- **Surfstats Log Analyzer**: A 14-day trial download is available at http://www.surfstats.com.

- **WebPosition Gold**: Another comprehensive analyzer product that is available for free trial download. Find it at http://www.webposition.com.

Developing a Brand

From a flying window to a leather "swoosh," brand names and brand logos can mean immediate customer recognition. If you want to be considered among the favored places to do business, you'll want to establish *your* mark.

Though branding can be relatively simple, big businesses spend millions upon millions of dollars each year hoping to establish the next big name in consumer goods. Oftentimes, millions upon millions of dollars go down the drain on failed efforts. So keep your sights appropriate to the immediate size of your business, but don't be afraid to dream a bit about the potential for your piece of the pie.

Making a Name for Yourself

To start, your business needs a name. According to some of the greatest minds in marketing, a good business (or product) name has the following characteristics:

- It defines the benefit of your product or service.

- It is easy to remember.

- It is not too similar to established business names or brands.

- It isn't too generic nor is it too specialized.

- It differentiates you from other businesses or competitors.

- It is multinational.

Once you decide on a name, see if you can secure a Web domain name for it. This is tough since so many domain names have been snapped up, often for the mere purpose of selling ownership later. Visit InterNIC's Web site at http://rs.internic.net to determine if the domain name you have your heart set on is still available. If the exact name isn't available, experiment with different spellings or formations, but don't create such an esoteric URL that customers won't remember how to enter it to find your site.

AuctionWatch.com has more!

Get going on your merchant Web site—read AW's extensive seller tip, Registering a Domain Name, at http://www.auctionwatch.com/awdaily/tipsandtactics/sel-domain.html

Now you need a logo or a brand mark. This is strictly extra credit, but a well-designed emblem can help establish your business in the minds of your customers. Be it cute, clever, professional, or personable, your special design can be a great marketing tool.

And don't forget: whatever name, logo, or brand mark you decide on, be sure to have it clearly visible on your Web site, your auction listings, and all correspondence with your customers.

Key Watch Points

- If you've maxed out the potential of the auction sites but still feel there is more opportunity to grow your business, it's time to consider developing your merchant presence.

- Be sure you're ready (and able) to commit to establishing your own business, otherwise customers will see yours as a half-hearted attempt and will quickly dismiss you.

- Tap the Web to take advantage of the best place today to start up, develop, and advertise your business.

- Take the time to profile your customers to ensure your business slant is exactly what folks are looking for.

- Use one of the many Web analyzers to determine how effective your site is at attracting and retaining potential customers who come by to visit.

- Make the effort to develop a meaningful and memorable name and branding for your business. It should be the sort of thing that really sticks in people's minds and brings them back for more.

CHAPTER 14

Customer Support: The Next Level

Level: **Advanced**

Reader: **Seller**

Ask any online auction-goer and you'll learn that one of the key differences among auction sites, as well as among other online merchants, often boils down to customer service. Some bemoan the total lack of service at one site while others praise the high-quality assistance at another. In fact, customer service has become so important to buyers that many will cite it as the deciding factor when considering which sites to patronize.

Whether you're a seller at an auction site or a business owner hosting your own sales site, customer service isn't difficult to achieve—and, with just a bit more effort, superior customer service can be easier to deliver than you may think. Of course, this leaves many wondering, "Why doesn't *everyone* offer stellar service?"

The Essentials of Excellent Customer Service

Though you should move with your customers' needs and desires, it's really not necessary to bend over backward to provide excellent service. Effective customer service is like effective business: often, the simpler the better.

Know Who Your Target Customers Are and What They Want

You can't be all things to all customers, so don't try. Focus on a defined group of people, and give the people what they want!

Make Good on Your Promises

Whether it's product availability, delivery, or any of your sales policies, be sure you do what you've stated you'd do.

Be Responsive

Dead air in cyberspace is unsettling for all customers, especially newcomers. Be available for communication and be sure to communicate quickly and clearly when a customer has a question, a comment, or a complaint.

Listen to Your Customers

Hear what they have to say and learn from it. They're telling you what they want from a seller and what they'll be willing to pay for.

Show them You Care

Take an interest in their needs, send that little thank-you note, or tell them of a related event or business that might appeal to their interests. They'll recognize that you understand and acknowledge them beyond a single business transaction.

Define Customer Satisfaction

Now, when you discuss customer satisfaction, your goal is to understand what it truly is:

- Customer satisfaction is determined by the customers, not by the seller or service provider.

- It is the customers who decide which site is best, which product is best, and which method is best.

- Satisfied customers are the ones that are served the way *they* like to be served, not the way you think they'd like to be served.

- Customers want to be treated with dignity and respect and want to feel like you're happy they've visited your business.

How Do You Stack up?

As you're considering those points, ask yourself the following questions about what your customers might experience when dealing with you and your business site:

- Does your business live up to its promises in regard to products, services, and ease of use?

- Can customers find what they're looking for (or determine whether you have what they're looking for) quickly at your place of business?

- Can customers serve themselves at your business or must they place a phone call or send an e-mail request in order to do business with you?

- Is the information about your product or service adequate to allow customers to buy with immediate confidence?

- Can customers easily find out more about you before deciding to do business at your site?

- Do customers have options in how they communicate with you or arrange payment? Customers don't like being cornered into limited methods of doing business (the perception is you've aligned the business to suit your needs, not theirs).

Sellers that take advantage of AW's Post Sale Management tool within Auction Manager can offer their customers a range of payment, shipping, and insurance options. Learn more at http://www.auctionwatch.com/help/acp/psmtool-howto.html

The Extra Mile

But how 'bout those touches that help customers remember your name and your site? Here are a few suggestions that could help customers enjoy doing business with you beyond simply buying your goods:

- Provide commentary on your site that speaks to the sort of items you're selling and to the customers who will be interested in them. Write a "column of the week" that discusses topics of interest to your customers or that better explains who you are.

- Establish a mailing list where your customers can "opt in" to be notified of future acquisitions or special sales events.

- Survey your customers to determine how well they like your site and your business practices. Many won't tell you if they have a problem but most will be eager to speak up when invited to.

- Keep a customer list and consider sending out special notes at the holidays. It's a simple thing to do but it really shows your customers that you're organized and pleasant to do business with.

Have you tried AW's Customer Management tool within Auction Manager? It allows you to establish and manage an ongoing sales relationship with your customers. Learn more at http://www.auctionwatch.com/help/acp/crmtool-howto.html

E-mail Support

This is perhaps one of the easiest customer support tools to put in place. If done right, it provides your customers an easy way to contact you, while giving *you* an opportunity to tend to other aspects of your business without constant interruption.

Following are the key benefits of establishing e-mail support for your business:

- Customers can make contact with you any time of day, any time of year.

- You can establish a routine to manage daily inquiries, instead of being interrupted when you when you least expect it.

- E-mail correspondence gives you time to research a customer's question, check your available inventory, or carefully consider how you'll respond to best satisfy the customer's query.

- With e-mail correspondence, you can attach images or other informative material that will be useful to your customer (but be sure to scan for viruses both outgoing and incoming).

- You can easily provide an e-mail link to a dedicated customer inquiry mail node on your Web site.

- You can inform customers of your e-mail reply turnaround time (no more than 48 hours, please) at the moment they send a message.

- E-mail correspondence is cheap and easy for both you and your customers.

These days, many people send more e-mail than they do regular (snail) mail. It's fast, it's efficient, and for you it's good for business.

AuctionWatch.com has more!

See AW's extensive seller tip, Wording Auction Emails during and after your transactions. Find it at http://www.auctionwatch.com/awdaily/tipsandtactics/sel-email.html

Phone Support

Though it's not always the most convenient for you, there are times you'll need to provide live phone support for your customers. This largely depends on the sort of products you'll be selling. If you're dealing in high-value, obscure, or rare items, it could be best to provide a phone number for customers to talk with you.

- To best support your business without interrupting the rest of your life (and the lives of others with whom you share living space), establish a dedicated business number.

- Understand and exercise proper phone courtesy. Remember, when you answer that phone you'll only have the one opportunity to make a good first impression.

- Answer your phone by identifying your business name; customers don't like hearing "Hullo" and wondering if they got a wrong number.

- Politely ask why the customer felt the need to call. Was there a problem with your site or the information on it or did they simply wish to speak with a live person?

- If you can't answer someone's question right away, get their phone number and offer to call back a little later.

- Keep your business line open as much as possible. Most customers won't have patience for constant busy signals and will proceed to shop somewhere else.

Business Hours

Even though online auctions are open 24/7, don't think that you should compete with that. In the interest of good work/life balance and good physical health, you need to establish which hours and days you'll be working and which you'll be resting. Your customers won't expect you to be perpetually on duty—but that doesn't mean you have to give the impression you're not always open for business.

- Advertise phone hours on your Web site or within the body of your auction listings so customers will know when you're available to talk.

- Offer alternate forms of communication, such as e-mail or fax, so customers can communicate when it's convenient for *them*.

- Hook up an answering machine to your business line or establish a voice-mail account for that number so customers can leave messages when you're away or unavailable to pick up their calls. Be sure to call back, though.

- Let customers know in advance when you'll be away from your business in cases of extended travel or vacations.

Satisfaction Guaranteed

Perhaps the sharpest double-edged sword you'll face in your business is a claim of "100 percent satisfaction guaranteed." It's truly the best policy for encouraging new customers to do business with you. At the same time, you may fear that such a policy will open the door to unscrupulous buyers who will try to make a doormat of you. The good news is that you can provide a policy that treats the customer like royalty *and* keep yourself from feeling like a fool.

To establish a successful guarantee program, be sure to do the following:

- Post your guarantee plainly and clearly on your business site and within your auction listings.

- Explain exactly what you guarantee, but don't get caught up in a lot of small print and conditional text. The best policy is "100 percent guaranteed, full refund if not fully satisfied."

- Be friendly in all dealings, especially in times of expressed customer dissatisfaction.

- Be genuinely concerned if a customer raises a complaint or feels the need to exercise your guarantee policy. This could tell you something about how you're positioning your products or perhaps how you're potentially misleading customers.

- Always work to make the sale right. Ask if the customer wants a replacement, credit, or a refund. Options allow customers to choose what's best for them. The best sellers are those who can leave a customer feeling confident about having dealt with them and eager to come back even if a deal fell apart or a product failed to satisfy.

AuctionWatch.com has more!

Read AW's extensive seller tip on the pluses and minuses of offering refunds and guarantees, at http://www.auctionwatch.com/awdaily/tipsandtactics/sel-refunds.html

Seller, Protect Thyself

That all sounds fine from the customer's standpoint, but how can you be sure you won't be a target for false claims, switch-and-return scams, and generally having your good business nature taken for granted? Well, it's a very fine line, but you can satisfy customers while still protecting yourself in the process.

- Anticipate your customers' needs and goals to determine if they appear as good prospects or potential sources of discontent.

- Try to pick up on your customers' attitudes as you begin to arrange a sale with them—are they pleasant and agreeable to your products and policies or are they immediately taking exception to some of your business stipulations?

- Establish policies in which you can explain how *both* of you will be protected; never appear suspicious of a customer but explain your need, as a businessperson, to protect your interests.

- Beware customers who seem overly interested in your return policies—they may not be planning to stick with the deal.

AuctionWatch.com has more!

Read AW's extensive seller tip, Avoiding the Buy & Switch, during your transactions: http://www.auctionwatch.com/awdaily/tipsandtactics/sel-switch.html

- Don't be afraid to turn a customer away if you feel doubtful about the final outcome—explain that you don't feel you can meet the customer's needs and that the transaction should be avoided.

In the end, expect that a 100 percent satisfaction guaranteed policy will cost your business from time to time. Whether it's claims of broken merchandise, lost packages, or a change of heart, sometimes your best efforts will go unrewarded. Typically, this is a cost of doing business and will be the minority of your dealings. However, just the fact that you are willing to offer such a guarantee can often bring in business, since it shows your commitment to fair, honest, and customer-driven business tactics.

Key Watch Points

- Today, customer service has become a key differentiator among those who attract one-time customers and those who keep them coming back for more.

- Employ simple customer service programs and policies—they cost very little to implement but can spell additional profits for your business.

- Make use of e-mail correspondence, phone support, and established business hours to allow your customers to get in touch with you.

- Seriously consider adopting a 100 percent satisfaction guaranteed policy for your business, then take the appropriate steps to fully define it, stand behind it, and uphold it to the protection of both your customers and your business.

CHAPTER 15

Register, Report, and Deduct: The Pros and Cons of Being a Business

Level: *Advanced*

Reader: *Buyer and Seller*

Establishing your own online business can provide freedom and flexibility you might never have dreamed possible. Though it's a lot of work, running your own show puts you in control and gives you the opportunity to explore new ways to make a living. But don't forget there is still much of the real world to contend with and, to small business owners, that means licensing, registration, and tax liability.

Though you may hold a certain disdain for bureaucracy, resistance is futile. Knowledge, however, is essential. You need to understand what your business requirements and liabilities are if you're to stay in business and out of trouble with your local and federal government agencies. Despite the many regulations you'll encounter, government interest isn't all burdensome—there are also small business assistance programs and exclusions that can help your business grow and prosper.

But first . . . the disclaimer (you knew it was coming): The information provided here is intended to guide you toward a better understanding of some of the elements of legally establishing your business and reporting your business activity to government agencies (such as the IRS). The rules differ from state to state and even town to town, so please consult the proper agencies as well as a CPA to be sure you fully understand the limitations and liabilities as they might pertain to your own business.

There, that wasn't so bad.

Licensed for Business

Though people often conduct their occasional auction activities without one, in many states the act of buying items wholesale for the purpose of reselling them online or elsewhere requires a valid resale license (also known as a *seller's permit*). Licenses can be required at the city level, county level, or with other states. Since the requirements can vary significantly from state to state, it's wise to visit your local state's business administration home page. Start by visiting the Small Business Administration (SBA) site at: http://www.sba.gov.

There you'll find links to your state's page, where you can get more information on the local business license regulation with which you'll need to comply.

But is registering your business simply an exercise in wading through red tape? Actually, no. Though you may not see the need to register when your business first starts up, there are a number of services and protections to be gained as your business grows. Consider these, for example:

- Business structure assistance

- Business tax liabilities and advantages

- Business insurance

- Trademark registration and protection

- Patent protection and assistance

- Copyright protection and assistance

In addition, according to the SBA, failure to comply with business licensing and adherence to regulations could leave you legally unprotected, expose you to penalties, and generally put your business at risk of dissolution.

AuctionWatch.com has more! _____

Be sure to read AW's extended seller tip on getting properly licensed, at http://www.auctionwatch.com/awdaily/tipsandtactics/sel-license.html

Capital Gains on Auction Sales

Wherever you make a profit taxes must be paid. While you may well consider skirting the issue of paying taxes related to your garage sale, your baby-sitting, and your appearance at collector's shows, understand that your state and federal government isn't as likely to be so permissive when it comes to online auctions. Given the billions of dollars in e-revenues generated by online auctions, the tax collectors are getting more than curious about who's making how much and how much of that the government can tap into.

If you're doing steady business at online auctions and are seeing profits on the income you generate over and above the cost invested in the items you're selling, you are realizing capital gains. More plainly put:

- A capital gain (or loss) is the difference between what capital asset cost you (known as the *basis*) and what you got when you sold the asset.

- A capital asset is any item you have acquired for personal or investment purposes, including your china cabinet as well as your business inventory.

- If your total capital gains exceed your total capital losses, you must pay tax on the difference.

- If your total capital losses exceed your total capital gains, you are eligible to deduct the losses—up to a published annual limit—from your other realized income.

- Capital gains and losses are classified as short-term (the asset was held for one year or less before sale) or long-term (the asset was held longer than one year) and could be taxed differently.

- Capital gains and losses should be reported on Form 1040, Schedule D—Capital Gains and Losses.

Naturally, you'd prefer to see your capital gains exceed your capital losses, and the government would like that too. When you're successful in business, you must share the wealth with the IRS.

AuctionWatch.com has more!

Don't miss AW's comprehensive seller tip on reporting auction income, at http://www.auctionwatch.com/awdaily/tipsandtactics/sel-reporting.html

How Big Is Your Business?

One of the many complicating factors about how your business income will be taxed depends on how large your business is and how you have formally established it. Not all businesses are taxed the same since not all businesses are structured and operate the same. Understand the different types of business organization to best suit your business goals as well as to make the best of the tax laws.

Sole Proprietorship

If yours is a one-person show without any special corporation designation, you fall into this business type. Taxes on sole proprietorships are identical to individual income taxes—you and your business are considered one and the same. But that doesn't mean business income is just like salary; you'll be responsible for paying self-employment taxes, which include roughly an additional 15 percent liability for Social Security and Medicare. Here, you'll use the Form 1040 Schedule C (Business Income and Expenses) as well as Schedule SE (Self-Employment).

Partnership

Work with another person and claim it as such without claiming corporate status and you'll fall into this business category. Interestingly, taxes on this sort of business model are treated similarly to those on a sole proprietorship: two self-employed individuals working a business but not *employees* of the business will file individual tax returns based on their share of the income of the partnership. The business, not claimed as a separate entity, is not taxed. The partnership files its business activity information via Form 1065 Schedule K-1. The partners, then, report their personal income and tax liability using Form 1040 Schedule E.

C Corporation

Once you officially name your corporation and go through the registration process that lets you include *Inc.*, *Corp.*, or *Ltd.* along with it, you qualify as a C corporation. A corporation is taxed as a separate entity by way of the *corporate income tax*. For corporations, taxable income can be affected by how much the owners withdraw in the form of salary, benefits, or dividends. In addition, corporate income can be subject to *double taxation,* that is, any profit a corporation claims is taxed; if the owners withdraw it for their own use, that profit is then considered *dividends* and will be taxed as personal income on the owners' individual tax returns. A corporation files an individual return using Form 1120 using tax brackets that are different from individual (personal) tax filings.

S Corporation

This is more like a partnership in that the income is taxed as if it were all claimed by the owner—which may be just one person or a group of people. The corporation reports activity via Form 1120S Schedule K-1 and the owners file Schedule E to report their share of the business profits.

Limited Liability Company

The LLC structure is available to businesses with two or more owners, who have the liberty to choose if they will be taxed as a partnership (using Form 1065 Schedule K-1 and Schedule E) or as a corporation.

Clearly, the government hasn't made determining which business model is best very easy to do. Be sure to consult a tax professional for an accurate assessment of your business, its potential, and the best choice for business declaration. Then check with your state to determine any limitations or special fees that might be levied on different business structures. And visit the IRS Web site at http://www.irs.gov/forms_pubs/index.html for a more than generous dose of documentation and explanation of the different tax forms and application to the different business structures.

Social Security Tax

I mentioned this under sole proprietorship, but make a special note that—as a self-employed individual earning income—you are responsible for certain federal payments that most employers manage for you. The total is calculated as a fixed percentage of your business income as follows:

- **Social Security liability**. 12.4 percent of a base amount (a ceiling amount stated by the government). You should be so lucky as to get anywhere near the ceiling these days.

- **Medicare liability**. 2.9 percent of *all* profit your business realizes.

Self-employment tax often comes as a rude surprise to those who conduct auctions or a separate business as a sideline activity. Remember, these are the deductions your regular employer splits with you, paying half while you pay the other half. But when it's your own business, you're responsible for the whole amount.

Business Deductions

Naturally, it takes money to make money. Whenever your business incurs expenses in its striving for profit, those are probably deductible costs that can offset a portion of your net income (that is, your receipts less the cost of the goods you sold). Though some consider taking business deductions as sly and maybe even illegal—which occasionally it can be, if the deductions aren't legit—most who aren't already aware are surprised and pleased to learn the different expenditures that can be justifiably deducted from their business proceeds.

To begin, understand the normal business expenses that you should be deducting from your net income:

- Supplies

- Office furniture

- Office equipment (PC, fax, printer, phone, and so on)

- Business-related postage costs

- Training and other business-related educational expenses

- Business counseling fees

- Tax preparation fees

- Rent or mortgage interest

- Phone and Internet connection fees

- Legal fees

- Bad debts (unpaid sales)

- Business travel costs (transportation, meals, lodging, entertainment)

Be sure to consider other expenses that you incur as part of keeping your business alive and thriving, and consult your tax adviser to see what additional deductions you may be letting slip through your fingers (and into Uncle Sam's hands).

Tax Shelters

Though the name has oft been maligned as a business's loophole to evade tax liability, tax shelters or breaks are very much legitimate and each business owner should make the most of them.

The goal of a tax shelter is to reduce your business's net income by deflecting some monies to recognized state and federal investment programs. As you operate your business, consider some prime tax reduction opportunities.

Retirement Plans

Many financial advisers will encourage small business owners to take advantage of income deferment programs such as IRAs, Roth-IRAs, and Keogh Plans. The money you filter to these investment accounts can be deducted from your business income prior to taxation.

Family Employment

If you've got your under-18 kids lending you a hand in your business, consider *employing* them and paying them for their efforts. The money you pay them is nontaxable up to an established ceiling amount. Those wages can help reduce your business income and the tax liability that will accompany it.

Business Insurance and Other Protections

Your business is a profit-making machine and it deserves to be properly protected. Business insurance, therefore, should be considered to ensure that you don't lose the farm in the case of an unforeseen incident.

Property Insurance

Many home business operators don't realize their homeowner's insurance fails to cover any potential business losses as a result of fire, natural disaster, or theft or vandalism. Some homeowner's policies only cover personal property to a maximum value (regardless of actual value) and many have exclusions that would render your property uninsured if not at your principal place of residence (such as portable electronics or off-site storage).

Liability Insurance

Though your home is usually covered if personal visitors hurt themselves on your property, business visitors may not be covered.

Employee Insurance

If your business has grown and you've got a staff helping you run the shop, be sure to look into the following employee-related protections:

- Unemployment coverage
- Workers' compensation
- Disability insurance

Miscellaneous Insurance

Don't forget the other types of coverage that can help protect your business.

- Auto insurance (business vehicles)
- Business interruption coverage
- Health insurance
- Product liability insurance
- Employer practices liability

Again, take the time to consult the SBA site to learn more about business insurance options and how you can determine which coverage is best for your business.

Charging Sales Tax

One of the most active discussions related to online auction sales concerns the levying of sales tax. In general, businesses are required to charge state sales tax for all retail sales made within their state of residence (or the state of business residence). However, with online auctions easily and regularly spanning multiple states, the levying of sales tax could be quite burdensome.

The Internet Freedom Act of 1998 was passed to waive the need for out-of-state sales taxes for Internet sales. That effectively solved the interstate tax collection problem (at least for now) but there is still the in-state tax requirement to contend with. Technically, sellers with valid business licenses are responsible for collecting and remitting taxes on retail sales made within their state of business.

AuctionWatch.com has more!

Find out what the possibility of increased Internet taxation means for online auction buyers and sellers in AW's hard-hitting report "To Tax or Not to Tax?"

htthttp://www.auctionwatch.com/awdaily/features/tax/index.html

Why is this such a hot topic within the online auction communities? Many buyers complain that some sellers are falsely collecting sales tax on Internet sales. Therefore, before you try to glean an extra buck or two on an online sale, be prepared for a buyer to ask you to provide your business license number for verification. If you don't have one, you could be accused of tax fraud. (And if you have one and aren't using it to report taxes, you're in real trouble if the state finds out.)

Key Watch Points

- Obtaining a business license is required of most valid businesses, depending on local and state regulations.

- Business owners have several ways to organize their businesses and should consider the benefits and liabilities of each business structure as they decide how they will establish themselves.

- As a business owner, be sure you understand the tax liability on your business income.

- Don't overlook any of the legal deductions that you can (and should) take advantage of to legitimately reduce your tax liability.

- Sales taxes should be collected by sellers who complete in-state sales and hold a valid business license that requires them to collect and remit state sales taxes.

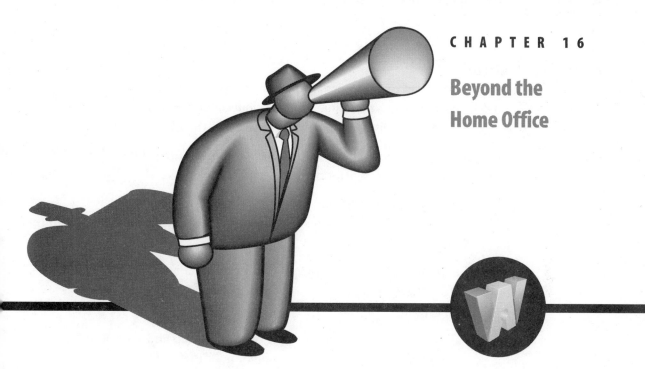

CHAPTER 16

Beyond the Home Office

Level: *Advanced*

Reader: *Seller*

Don't be surprised if one day, while you're busily working your business—listing items, updating an online inventory, collecting payment, and making shipments—you suddenly experience a feeling of limitation. Whether you feel the need to spread out or the desire to balance your business between cyberspace and the real world, you might find yourself considering breaking the confines of your home office.

Seldom has there been a better general environment for entrepreneurs or a more general acceptance of the "little businessperson" offering the buying public an alternative to the staid ways of big businesses. If you've come to realize the grander potential for you and your business, consider what may lie in front of you by way of additional opportunities to grow your business.

What's Your Motivation?

Though it's nothing you want to jump into without careful consideration, other sellers have cited many different reasons for expanding their business empires:

- Their business has grown but their business space hasn't, resulting in a cramped and inefficient operation.

- They're working as fast as they can but can't keep up with customer demand and sales activity; they need to expand and take in more help just to keep from losing sales.

- Their local zoning laws prevent them from operating a recognizable business from their homes so they need to establish a legal "business location."

- They've always dreamed of running their own little shop and now have the capital and customer base to make a go of it.

- They're looking for even more opportunity to attract customers and wish to establish a visible presence in their community.

- They need to get out a little; they can no longer stand month after month of seeing only a computer monitor as they conduct business.

Whatever the reason, many sellers ponder branching out into new avenues to bolster their business. Again, it's not a step to be taken lightly or ventured into capriciously—it *can* boost your business but it can also kill it if not executed carefully.

A Final Checklist

To be sure you're truly ready and able to broaden your physical horizons, take each of the following into consideration:

- Assess your true motivation for leaving your home office: be sure it's due to a solid business need and not a personal or emotional whim.

- Be certain your business is safely and consistently operating at a profit.

- Determine if and how your present business will be interrupted as you set up a new headquarters and what financial impact you will face.

- Understand the actual costs of relocating (moving expenses, setup expenses, rent, utilities, and so on) and figure out if your present and future income will cover the costs while still providing an acceptable profit.

- Determine if there is truly a better venue that will help your business grow (if it merely stays the same, it's probably not worth the relocation costs).

- Determine if moving your business will interfere with your operations so much that your income will drop more than you can tolerate while you're adapting to the new location.

- Be ready and willing to delegate some of your current business activities if growth entails bringing helpers on board.

- Be sensitive to your customers and their acceptance of a relocation. Can they still contact you as easily? Will they benefit from being able to visit you in a physical location?

Before You Go, Is There a Better Alternative?

If you've carefully considered your needs and motivations for relocating your business, give the prospect one more close look. Remember that profit is your incentive for being in business (it is, isn't it?) and you should continually be on the lookout to do more with your business for less. Therefore, before you call the movers and begin packing up your office, think about different alternatives.

Zoning

Though you may be subject to zoning restrictions on running a home-based business, be sure you understand what *is* allowed from your home location and see if you can work to those allowances. Consider how you can stay below the radar in regard to customer visits, pick-up and delivery activity, and on-site helpers (employees) to the point that your operations are allowable by local law and still have room for your income to grow.

Merchandise Receipt

Some neighbors could dislike the constant coming and going of UPS and Postal Service vehicles and could raise issues with your city about your home business. Rather than aggravate those around you, consider using a mail delivery service (such as a P.O. box or as offered by Mail Boxes Etc.) to receive your deliveries, which you can retrieve later.

Inventory Storage and Shipment

If it's wall-to-wall, floor-to-ceiling inventory that has you cramped, consider renting storage or warehouse space. And, depending on the sorts of items you'll be selling, you could consider employing a fulfillment company that will receive orders and ship product for you. Many manufacturers, wholesalers, and distributors will also work with *drop-shippers* that will even own the financial investment in the inventory; all you do is market the merchandise and manage the orders.

Travel to the Trade Shows

If you want to get out and mingle with more customers face to face, consider visiting trade shows, exhibitions, and consignment stores where you can set up shop for a day, a weekend, or however long they'll host you and your merchandise. Many collectibles sellers travel the trade show circuit to keep current with other buyers and sellers as well as to establish a physical-world relationship with at least some of their customers. Though at any of these venues you'll have expenses (rent, travel, setup), the costs are extremely controllable by means of establishing how long you and your merchandise will be "on the road." And, if you're new to the trade show and event circuit, be sure to visit http://www.tscentral.com, an incredible resource that will quickly have you up to speed and up and running in the trade show world.

Outside Office

But if your business truly needs to spread out, consider establishing an outside-the-home business office. First determine if it's just administrative space that you need. Sometimes, your business productivity can suffer due to common "home interruptions:" a television set, friends calling, neighbors popping by, and kids and pets running about. It may be that a separate place is all you need to focus on managing your business. After all, many business owners find they can get far more done if away from domestic distractions, but they still don't want their customers to be able to visit them in person.

If you're considering an office space, keep these points in mind:

- Find an office space that is relatively nearby, to limit time lost in the commute.

- Find an office in a quiet part of town where other, more active businesses or traffic activity won't distract you.

- Find an office *upstairs*—many private-office-dwellers note that an upstairs office is less likely to invite misguided visitors or delivery personnel looking for so-and-so's suite.

- Find an office that has all the amenities you'll need, including multiple phone lines, plenty of electrical outlets, adequate lighting. Remember that you'll need to pay for office amendments to fit your business needs.

- Find a reasonably priced office. It probably won't be the fanciest, but administrative tasks don't require waterfalls and metal sculptures.

AuctionWatch.com has more! _____

Read AW's extensive seller tip on setting up your auction office, at http://www.auctionwatch.com/awdaily/tipsandtactics/sel-office.html

Physical Storefront

Some sellers have already begun serving customers at their home offices. Their clientele visit from time to time to make a purchase in the physical realm. Some sellers, in fact, enjoy a steady stream of customers that come in to shop and have shown there is still appeal for shopping "in person."

Foot traffic is still one of the best forms of advertising and branching out into a physical storefront can offer the additional boost your business can profit from. Besides, as mentioned before, owning the little shop on the corner is the dream of many entrepreneurs.

Square Footage

How much room will you need to host a successful store? Remember, moving out should improve your business's appeal. If you like your store cozy, just be sure it's not too cramped. If you dream of truly expanding, be sure you've got the inventory to support it. Avoid the appearance of a virtually empty store with a few items over in the far corner.

Cost

Operating a store can be costly, starting with the landlord who rents you the space. Then factor in the cost of utilities, maintenance, and additional advertising (those neon "open" signs are quite expensive). Be cost conscious, as with any other business expansion, and be sure not to take the cost of any aspect of running a business lightly.

Location, Location . . . (You Know)

What will make a good location for your little piece of the market? Think about activity around the site: is there enough walk-by or drive-by traffic to steer new customers your way? Think about amenities: is it a safe area that's clean and has adequate parking? Consider accessibility for physically disadvantaged customers—sometimes such access is a requirement to being allowed to open a retail site. How about your competition—are you moving in next to or near an established business that's sure to siphon off customers before they can get to *your* door?

Neighborhood Input

Just as you'd scout around when looking for a home, do the same sort of scouting for a business location. If you find a space available, talk to other businesses nearby or in the same building. Determine how long they've been in business, what kind of customer traffic they receive (and it's a good idea to check on the latter claims by hanging around the area for a half-day), and how the area seems to serve their business. You can usually learn a lot about how your business might fare by talking to a businessperson who has already set up shop.

And before you decide a physical storefront is what will rocket your business to the next level of success and profitability, consider how you'll make the transition into your business's new home. You'll want your shop to be different from all the others and to provide services (as well as merchandise) that other shop owners simply are not offering.

Give Your Store a Personality

Just as you've worked so hard to develop your own business personality online, understand how similar thematic approaches will work to draw people into your store. As an example, if you'll specialize in books, provide seating and maybe even a pot of fresh coffee for folks to sit down and ponder a few of your products. Develop an environment that makes visiting your store more of an experience rather than simply a "point of exchange" (much as you developed your Web site).

Give Your Customers First-rate Service

Just as you worked to provide stellar service online, understand that many customers these days are tired of being herded about in mega-stores, clutching a number and generally being regarded as such. Be enthusiastic when you greet visitors to your store, be helpful but don't be a shadow, and be alert for when they might have a question or comment about your merchandise. Get to know your customers, find out what they want in the way of products and information, and keep in contact with them when you uncover an item or tidbit of knowledge that they'll be sure to appreciate (and pay for).

Be Sure Your Store's Online

No, not just having a companion Web site to your store (which you should have), but consider bringing a PC into your store—one that customers could potentially use. If you'll continue your online auctions and sales, steer customers to the PC where they can view what you have up for bid. Who knows, they might never have found that auction otherwise—and you've just bridged the gap between your cybersales and physical sales.

Small Business Loans

Assuming you've been making a go of it out of your own pocket (and hopefully through the reinvestment of your business income), you're apt to find your ability to successfully expand your business directly related to the amount of money you have to invest. Unless your home-based, Net-based endeavors have generated a financial windfall, figure that getting out into the physical business world will require a bit of financial assistance.

So what kinds of financial help can you expect to find? That's the good news— there are quite a variety of loans and loan programs aimed at helping small business owners make a bigger splash in their market.

Personal Loans

You can fund your business expansion (or start-up) on your good name. Savings and Loan institutions as well as commercial banks regularly grant personal loans for business ventures, though it's usually not important to them *what* you intend to use the money for—just as long as you can pay it back. Expect to provide full disclosure of your credit history as well as your employment history and current status. And remember that personal loans often carry a higher interest rate than commercial loans, so you'll want to be able to pay it off quickly.

Line of Credit

Many banks and credit unions offer access to money that you can use much the same as you do your credit card (but typically at much lower interest rates). Check with your financial institution to see if they offer such a service and determine if the limit imposed will be enough to help your business surge ahead.

Commercial Bank Loans

And most business owners pursue the good old commercial loan. Commercial banks are getting much more liberal about granting such loans, depending, of course, on your business plan. However, commercial banks are more inclined these days to offer varying sizes of loans—you don't need to be borrowing

$75K in order to have your loan application taken seriously. Be on the look-out for loan offers from some of the larger commercial lending institutions such as Citibank, Wells Fargo, and American Express.

SBA Loans

Naturally, the Small Business Administration is the entrepreneur's advocate in building strong businesses. Visit the agency Web site or call its offices directly to learn about a wide variety of business loan programs it sponsors, such as SBA Express Loans, Capital Term Loans, and Microloans.

AuctionWatch.com has more!

Learn more about the SBA and its programs from Economic Development Specialist Gary Marshall in his AW Viewpoint column, "SBA: Your Neighborhood Advocate," at http://www.auctionwatch.com/awdaily/viewpoint/speakout/so-sba.html

Are You a Good Loan Prospect?

Naturally, no one is too excited about laying out their needs and baring their soul to a lender. But if you think getting the capital you need for your business expansion means groveling on your knees in some banker's plush office, take heart—these days, lenders are looking for entrepreneurs who show good business sense and have achievable goals in mind. So, before you go looking for funding, do some preliminary work to help instill confidence in the people with the money you want.

Have a Well-prepared Business Plan in Hand

Lenders are eager to make interest on the loans they grant, but they're more interested in loaning money to individuals and businesses that have logic and facts to back up their loan requirements. Know exactly how much you'll need to borrow, show which expenses the loan will be covering, and why you'll need to incur those expenses (an obvious notion that loan applicants overlook more often than you'd think).

Have a Business Cash Flow Projection

You'll probably need a business adviser and accountant to help you with this one. Provide the lender with a projection of income and expenses you would expect of your business. Lenders want to see that the money they're ponying up won't be squandered on nonconsequential expenditures that won't garner income for your business. After all, they want to see a healthy income for your business so they'll know you'll be able to repay your loan.

Provide a Reasonable Loan Pay-off Plan

And from that previous point, again confer with an accountant to develop a reasonable pay-off plan. This shows lenders that you have thought further ahead than just the acquisition of initial capital and are as eager as they to see the loan paid back.

Have the Professional Advice You Need

If you invest in proper consultation, such as accountants, business advisers, and lawyers, you'll gain a better understanding of what taking out a business loan really means to you and your business. Professional advisers can help you understand the language and terms of different business loans and can help you choose the financial options that will serve you and your business best.

Collateral

That's right, lenders want some tangible assets that they can claim should you default on your loan. Lenders often need stocks, bonds, equipment, or structures that they can hold a claim against to "secure the loan." Often, you can remain the physical holder of the collateral and the claim will be lifted once you've paid off the loan amount.

Anything else? Yes. Also be prepared to offer up your personal profile—your credit history, your expertise in the field of business, and your sincerity that you're a good risk for this loan.

Key Watch Points

- Don't underestimate the potential of your business, and if you believe you're ready to go public, then perhaps there's a corner shop with your name above the door in your future.

- Be sure you carefully consider the move into a physical store front, though, with serious analysis of the initial costs, ongoing expenses, and potential benefit to your business.

- Consider in-between alternatives between cybersales and the physical world. An office or even a self-service storage space may be all you need, not a full-fledged store front.

- Choose a physical store front the same way you'd choose a home: understand the surroundings, the costs of occupancy, and the expected customer traffic you might see.

- Don't be afraid to ask for financial help. Though it will take some work, a personal or business loan might be the only thing standing in your way and keeping you from making your splash in the business world.

Glossary of Online Auction Lingo

Just like everything else on the Internet, online auctions have developed a language all their own. If you want to truly fit in, you need to talk like the natives. Most of the terms and phrases you'll encounter are traditional auction-speak. However, the *Net effect* has also spawned some language elements that you'll need to understand if you're going to keep pace with the rest of the community. Here's your chance to master the lingo.

A

Absentee Bidding. A bidding procedure that allows bidders to participate in physical auctions that they aren't able to attend. Generally, an absentee bid is submitted prior to the sale. Some brick-and-mortar auctions (especially high-end houses) accept absentee bids via their Web sites or via e-mail.

Absentee Bidder. A person who submits a written, oral, or electronic bid prior to a physical auction instead of attending it in person. This bid is understood as the bidder's *Maximum Bid*.

Absolute Auction. An auction in which the item up for sale is sold to the highest qualified bidder with no limiting conditions or preset final price requirements. Also known as a *Straight Auction* or an *Auction Without Reserve*.

Accounting of Sale. An auction summary issued to the seller by the auctioneer, detailing the financial aspects of the final sale.

Agent. A person who is authorized to act on behalf of another individual or entity during a public auction.

Aggregating, Aggregators. The method of performing multi-site searches using a third-party search engine to assist individuals in finding what they want without visiting the sites individually. Aggregators are the parties that perform such searches; the term also refers to the custom search programs they have developed.

Agreement. An expression of mutual assent by two or more parties on a given proposition. Refer to *User Agreement*.

Appraisal. The act or process of estimating an item's value via expert *Authentication* and comparative pricing in the open market. Appraised values can change as the marketplace valuation of an item increases or decreases.

"As Is". Selling an item without warranties in regard to its condition and fitness for a particular use. The buyer is responsible for judging the item's durability and lifetime. Also known as "as is, where is" and "in its present condition." Typically, this is a sign that no return privileges will be granted.

Auction. *n* (1) A method of selling a property in a public forum through open, competitive bidding. *v* (2) The act of putting an item up for sale in a competitive public auction.

Auction Block. The podium or platform from which an auctioneer conducts a physical auction. Online, refers to a "live listing" to be found in a listing *Category*. To place an item on the auction block means to make it available for competitive bidding.

Auction Listing Agreement. A contract executed by the auctioneer and seller, authorizing the auctioneer to conduct the sale. It also delineates the conditions of sale and the rights and responsibilities of each party. Also known as a *Listing Agreement*. Not to be confused with an online auction *User Agreement*.

Auction Plan. The itinerary for pre-auction, auction day, and post-auction activities, set by the auctioneer and seller.

Auction Subject to Confirmation. An auction in which the seller has set a reserve or minimum price for the item. This price must be met before the item can be sold. See *Reserve Price* and *Reserve Auction*.

Auction Value. The current price of a property during a competitive public auction. Also referred to as *Current Bid*.

Auction With Reserve. An auction in which the seller has set a minimum price for the item and reserves the right to accept or decline any and all bids that fail to meet that price condition. The minimum acceptable price may or may not be disclosed. Also known as an *Auction Subject to Confirmation* and *Reserve Auction*.

Auction Without Reserve. An auction in which the property is sold to the highest qualified bidder with no limiting conditions or minimum price. Also known as an *Absolute Auction* or *Straight Auction*.

Authentication. (1) The act or process of determining if an auction item is genuine and accurately represented by the seller. (2) A mark on an article that indicates its origin and authenticity.

B

Bid. An indication and offer on an item up for sale at a competitive public auction. Bids are typically made in predetermined *Bid Increments*.

Bid Cancellation. The cancellation of a bid from a buyer by a seller. During online auctions, sellers can cancel any bid if they feel uncomfortable about completing a transaction with a particular bidder.

Bid History. A historical list of bidding activity for a particular auction, viewable during or after the auction.

Bid Increment. The standardized amount an item increases in price after each new bid. Typically, the auction site or auctioneer sets the increment, though the increment can also increase in relation to the present high bid value.

Bid Retraction. The legitimate cancellation of a bid on an item by a buyer during an online auction.

Bid Rigging. An unlawful practice in which two or more people agree not to bid against one another in order to deflate the potential value of an item. See *Collusion*.

Bid Shielding. Posting extremely high bids (which are withdrawn at the last moment) to protect the lower bid of an earlier bidder, usually in cahoots with the bidder who placed the shielding bid.

Bid Siphoning. The practice of contacting bidders during an active auction and offering to sell them the same item they are currently bidding on, thus drawing bidders away from the legitimate seller's auction.

Bidder Search. An online search that will generate a list of items a user has bid on at an online auction service. Availability of this tool can vary from site to site.

Bidder's Choice. A method of sale in which the high bidder earns the right to select a particular item or property from a group of similar or identical ones.

Bidding. Offering to pay a specified amount of money for an item that is up for public auction.

Big-Ticket Item. An item with a bid of $5,000 or more.

Broker Participation. An arrangement in which a third-party broker registers potential bidders for an auction. Upon completion of the auction, the seller typically pays the broker a *Commission*.

Bulk Loading. Listing a group of different items in separate lots all at once using an online auction site's bulk loading tool or a specially designed third-party bulk loading tool.

Buyer's Broker. A broker hired to represent the buyer during an auction.

Buyer's Premium. An advertised percentage of the high bid or a flat fee, which is added to the high bid to determine the total price of the item or property. Most commonly assessed at High-End Auction houses.

Buying Up the Lot. The practice of buying everything on offer in a Dutch auction, rather than bidding on some smaller number of the items. This is typically done for resale.

Buy-It Price Auction. Auctions with immediate-sell prices that, when agreed to, will halt an auction and prevent any additional bidding. Also referred to as *Fixed-Price Auction* or Quick-Sell Auction.

C

Carrying Charges. The costs associated with holding an income-generating property. Examples include insurance, taxes, maintenance, and management.

Category. A logical item listing "bucket" where similar or related items can be found. Many categories are further broken down into more granular subcategories.

Category Listings. The categories in which an online auction site organizes its auctions.

Caveat Emptor. The Latin phrase for "let the buyer beware." It is a legal maxim, meaning that liability is transferred from the seller to the buyer in regard to the quality or condition of the item or property up for sale.

Collusion. An unlawful practice in which two or more people agree willfully and unfairly manipulate the final price of an auction item.

Commission. A fee paid by the seller to the auction site at the completion of an auction, calculated as a percentage of the final sale price. Also known as the *Final Value Fee (FVF)*.

Conditions of Sale. The legal terms that govern the conduct of a given auction. The conditions might include a *Reserve Price*, specific method of payment, or *Buyer Premium*.

Contact Information. The user information—generally name, street address, e-mail address, and phone number—provided when registering at an online auction site. All online auction sites require *Registered Users* to submit valid contact information.

Contract. A binding legal agreement between two or more persons or entities.

Cookie. A piece of information sent from a Web server to a Web browser that the browser software saves and then sends back to the server whenever the browser makes additional requests from the server. See also *Oreo*.

D

Deadbeat Bidding (Bidder). The failure to deliver payment on an item after securing the high bid in an online auction. Repeat deadbeat bidding will result in the indefinite suspension of a user from an online auction site.

DNF. Specific to eBay. Discuss Newest Features board. This is one of the more lively, if not cantankerous, message boards in the eBay auction community.

Due Diligence. The process of gathering information about the condition and legal status of items to be sold.

Dutch Auction. An auction format in which a seller lists multiple identical items for sale. Varying price determination methods exist. "authentic" Dutch Auctions determine price by lowering the price of the item until all units have been claimed (bid on); contemporary and online auctions use a format where all winning bidders pay the same price, which is the lowest successful bid. Often confused with the *Yankee Auction* format.

E

Emoticons. In-text icons created using common letters and punctuation marks to denote mood or attitude, for example.

: -) smiling face

: - (frowning face

: - P silly face with tongue sticking out

Escrow. Money held in trust by a third party until the seller makes delivery of merchandise to the buyer.

Estate Sale. The sale of personal property or real estate left by a person at the time of his or her death or incarceration.

F

Featured Auctions. An online auction site's most prominent auctions of the day. Featured Auction status typically incurs a separate and additional listing fee.

Feedback. One user's public comments about another user in regard to his or her auction dealings. Feedback comments cannot be removed or changed once submitted to an online auction site. Abbreviated as *fdbk* or *fk* (careful how you pronounce it).

Feedback Padding. Posting fraudulent positive feedback about a user or an auction, usually in an attempt to artificially raise a user's feedback rating or to offset the impact of negative feedback comments.

Final Value Fee (FVF). A fee paid by the seller to an auctioneer at the completion of an auction, calculated as a percentage of the final sale price. Also known as a *Commission*.

Fixed-Price Auction. See *Buy-It Price Auction*.

Flame. A harsh e-mail message or online *Public Forum* posting intended to incite an incident or verbally assault or publicly humiliate another person.

Flame War. A bitter volley of *Flames* exchanged in the heat of an online debate or argument.

FVF Refund Request. A request to an auction site for the crediting of a levied *Final Value Fee*. Usually granted in situations where an auction transaction is not completed (for example, because of a *Deadbeat Bidder*).

G

Grading. Documenting the physical condition of an item with a specific set of labels, such as "Mint" condition or "Poor" quality. Different items have different grading terms. For instance, trading cards are graded from "A1" to "F1," while coins are graded from "poor" to "perfect uncirculated."

H

Hammer Price. The final price of an item up for sale at a physical auction. The auctioneer acknowledges the high bid by striking the podium with a hammer or gavel.

High Bidder. The present or final bidder in an auction who has bid a higher price than any other bidder.

I

IMO, IMHO. The message board abbreviations for "in my opinion" and "in my honest (or humble) opinion."

Insertion Fee. A fee paid by the seller to the auction site in order to list an item for auction, calculated as a percentage of the opening bid or reserve price.

Item. The thing being auctioned. May be a single unit or a set of similar or even mixed objects, as long as the whole group is being sold as a unit to one buyer. Also called a Lot.

Item Lookup. An online search by item number. Every *Lot* on an online auction site is assigned an item number.

J

Jump Bid. A bid placed that significantly increases a current bid price well over the established next *Bid Increment*. Used to scare off other bidders who might not be able to contend at higher price levels.

K

Keyword Spamming. Deliberately placing a popular word in listing titles even though it is completely unrelated or irrelevant to the actual item being offered. Used to have items show up in the results of item searches.

Knock Down. Traditional auction term meaning to sell or receive payment from the high bidder.

Knock-Off. Slang term for an unlicensed reproduction or copy of an item that is made to appear as the real thing (such as brandname watches, sunglasses, handbags, and so on).

L

Listing Agreement. A contract executed by the auctioneer and seller, authorizing the auctioneer to conduct the sale. It also delineates the *Conditions of Sale* and the rights and responsibilities of each party. Also known as an *Auction Listing Agreement*.

LOL. The message board acronym for "laughing out loud."

Lot. The single item or group of items offered in a given auction listing

M

Market Value. The highest price a property will bring in the competitive, open market. See *Bidder Acknowledgment*.

Maximum Bid. The highest price a buyer will pay for an item, submitted in confidence to an online auction site's automated bidding system to facilitate *Proxy Bidding*. The system's electronic "proxy" will automatically increase the buyer's bid to maintain the high bid. The proxy bidding system will stop when it has won the auction or reached the *Maximum Bid*.

Minimum Bid Auction. An auction in which the auctioneer will accept bids only at or above a predisclosed price.

Minimum Opening Bid. The mandatory *Starting Price* for a given auction, set by the seller at the time of listing.

Multiseller Auction. Properties owned by multiple sellers, auctioned in a single event.

N

NARU'd. An auction site term to describe users whose memberships have been discontinued. NARU is the acronym for "not a registered user."

Neg. Short for "negative user feedback."

Net Cops. Auction users who actively seek out instances of fraud, such as shilling or bid shielding, to report to online auction sites.

Newsgroups. Public discussion forums that number in the thousands and are dedicated to specific topics of interest and conversation. See *Usenet*.

No-Sale Fee. A fee paid by the seller if the item on the block does not sell in a *Reserve Auction*.

NR. Short for "no reserve." This indicates in the item description line that the auction has no reserve price specified.

O

Opening Bid. The first bid offered by a bidder at an auction. Also known as the *Starting Price*.

Outbid. To submit a *Maximum Bid* that is higher than the one offered by another bidder. To "be outbid" indicates the reverse—someone who was the recognized high bidder has lost that status to someone else.

Outbid Notification. Communication sent via e-mail or sometimes wireless modes notifying a bidder of being outbid.

P

Pinkliner (aka "Pink" or "Pinkie"). Slang term (sometimes derogatory) used in the AuctionWatch.com Message Center to identify and accuse any particular poster of being in the employ (and potentially rallying for) a specific auction site and its policies. Liken to a "narc."

Private Auction. An auction in which the bidders are anonymous.

Proxy Bidding. To submit a confidential *Maximum Bid* to an online auction service's automated bidding system. The system's electronic "proxy" will automatically increase the buyer's bid to maintain the high bid. The proxy bidding system will stop when it has won the auction or reached the maximum bid.

Public Forum. On the Internet, a site, IP address, or mailnode where visitors can post topics for discussion.

Q

Quick-Sell Auction. See *Buy-It Price Auction*.

R

Registered User. A person who has registered as a member of an online auction service. All online auction services require registration prior to participation in an auction.

Re-listing. The re-listing of an item occurs when it has not sold within its allotted auction time. A fee is usually associated with re-listing.

Reserve Auction. An auction in which the seller has set a minimum selling price for the item and reserves the right to accept or decline any and all bids that have not met the established reserve. The minimum acceptable price may or may not be disclosed. Also known as an *Auction Subject to Confirmation* and *Auction With Reserve*.

Reserve Price. The minimum price a seller will accept for an item to be sold at a reserve auction. This amount may or may not be disclosed.

Retaliatory. The user term for retaliatory negative *Feedback*, posted by one user in response to another user's negative feedback.

S

S&H Charges. Shipping and handling charges.

Sealed Bid Auction. An auction in which confidential bids are submitted and opened at a predetermined place and time. Each bidder can place only one bid, so this format does not support competitive bidding.

Secure Server. A server that uses Secure Sockets Layer (SSL) encryption technology to protect users' credit card and other confidential information.

Seller List. A list of items a seller has put up for sale on an online auction site.

Seller Search. An automated search that retrieves a list of all the items a seller has put up for sale on an online auction site.

Shilling. Fraudulent bidding by the seller (using an alternate registration) or an associate of the seller in order to inflate the price of an item. Also known as *Bid Rigging* and *Collusion*.

Sniping. Bidding in the closing minutes or seconds of an auction to outbid other buyers.

Starting Price. The mandatory starting bid for a given auction, set by the seller at the time of listing.

Straight Auction. An auction in which there is no reserve and only one item is up for sale. This is the most common type of auction. The seller sets the opening bid and must respect the final price at the end of the auction.

T

Terms. The period of time that an agreement is in effect.

Terms of Service (TOS). A legally binding agreement that outlines an auction site's operations and policies. All registered users must agree to a site's terms before being allowed to use the service.

Tie Bids. Bids for exactly the same amount submitted by two or more buyers at the same time. In most *Straight Auctions*, the first bidder to have bid the amount will be declared the prevailing high bidder. Some online auction sites will award the win to the tie-bidder who was first to enter bidding on the item, regardless of when they're tying bid was submitted.

Troll. Someone who posts messages to public forums for the sake of stirring up tension, division, or confusion (a slang term). Also, a collectible plastic doll with grotesquely large features, wispy synthetic hair, and questionable gender.

Trustee. A person to whom property is legally committed in trust.

Trustee's Sale. A sale at auction by a trustee.

U

Upset Price. The bid amount that exceeds a seller's *Reserve Price*.

Usenet. An online hub of Newsgroups where visitors are invited to read public postings as well as post comments and observations of their own.

User Agreement. See Terms of Service.

User Discussion Boards. Public message boards where online auction site users can post their comments and questions.

User ID. A moniker that identifies a user while on an online auction site.

User Information. Personal data provided by a user when registering for an online auction site, including name, postal address, e-mail address, and phone number.

V

Verification. Confirming the identity and evaluating the condition of an item.

W

Winner's Curse. An oxymoron that indicates an overzealous bidder-*cum*-winner will be faced with paying their high bid—a bid perhaps placed during a moment of passion or excitement yet financially difficult for the bidder to honor.

Withdrawal. A bidder's withdrawal from an auction after having previously bid, either by way of *Bid Retraction* or as by yielding to a higher bidder.

X, Y

Yankee Auction. An auction in which a seller lists multiples of an identical item. Unlike a *Dutch Auction* (in which all winning bidders pay only the lowest successful winning bid amount), in a Yankee auction each winning bidder pays the exact amount actually bid.

Index

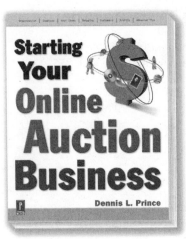
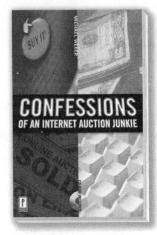

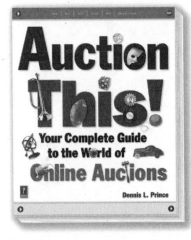